STRANDED NO WHERE

e a lake

Copyright © 2016 e a lake

All rights reserved.

ISBN: 1530743818

ISBN-13: 978-1530743810

This book is a work of fiction. The names, characters, places and incidents are products of the writer's imagination or have been used fictitiously and are not to be construed as real. Any resemblances to persons living or dead, actual events, locales or organizations are entirely coincidental.

All events portrayed are made up in the authors mind. As such, none are real. However, they are intended to give the reader pause to consider what a alternate future might look like. Further, the author intends to scare the living crap out of you. You're welcomed.

All rights reserved. No part of this book may be used or reproduced in any form whatsoever without written permission of the author.

Also by e a lake:

WWIV - In The Beginning,
WWIV - Hope in the Darkness,
WWIV - Basin of Secrets, and,

WWIV - Darkness Descends
(The Shorts - Book 1)

Coming Soon:

Surviving No Where (Book 2: The No Where Apocalypse)

WWIV - Darkness's Children
(The Shorts - Book 2)

For My Sons
Caleb, Micah and Ryan

If you find yourself here, I pray we'll find each other.
That by itself may make this bearable.
Lest we be truly *alone*.

- Bob Reiniger — No Where, MI

STRANDED NO WHERE

Year 23 WOP (without power)

I killed a man today. Another man, I should say. While it caused me no great pain to end his life, I can't say I found any particular joy in the act either.

That makes 14 in the past 22 years, maybe 23 now. Less than one a year; I'm not sure I've made mass murderer status yet or not. But in this miserable world without life or hope, I'm sure there are plenty of people who have killed more.

It happened like most of them did. Someone desperate, probably without a thing to eat or drink, shows up and wants to take what's mine. Once upon a time, I dreamt I'd shared with other folks. Now, well, they don't really seem like the sharing kind, in retrospect.

I was behind the cabin (I should really call it an over-sized shed) stacking green cut wood. That's all I do it seems, play with what Mother Nature made plentiful in this wilderness I call home. Some days it's felling trees, others I spend my time limbing, or cutting the large logs into workable sections. After that comes splitting, and that's back-breaking work.

Once split, the fresh cut stuff gets stacked along the back of my cabin/shed. Before I can do that, I have to move the stuff that has aged for a full year to the front. Rotate your wood; cut one year, burn last year's, stack this year's for drying. And that's where the trouble began.

By the time I saw this fellow, he was coming at me with an axe — my axe, more specifically. He was just screaming and foaming at the mouth. The foam is what made me think they'd all been hungry or thirsty. Not that I'm any sort of biology expert.

What he didn't know, what none of them have known thus far, is that they were attacking an armed man. See, I found the Glock 9mm that my dad left here in the middle of nowhere some number of years back. It claims, a stamp on the one side of the barrel, it's a model 19. I'll go with that; I don't know any different. The only thing I really know about it is that it's dull black with a few spots of rust, maybe seven inches long, and fires every time I pull the trigger.

My father had quite a collection of shells stashed here when I arrived. Most of them were 12-gauge shotgun shells, mind you. I don't own a shotgun, so I didn't have any use for them. But I figured out after a couple of years that other people were running out of ammo for their weapons. So after a full day's walk into the nearest town for some horse trading that would have made my old man smile and a full day's walk back, I finally got what I really needed: a case of 9mm handgun shells.

With almost 800 rounds for my gun, I went about learning how to use the damned thing. You see, I haven't even had a use for guns, much less a handgun. I live — check that, *lived* — in a big city. With almost eight million people in the Chicagoland area, I never found much need, much less room, for such a frivolous hobby.

My dad and older brother were the hunters. And up until the time I was 15, I spent some time in the woods as well. But at 15, I discovered basketball and girls. My growth spurt didn't go unnoticed by the local basketball coach, and my new letter jacket made me a stud among the frenzied female supporters.

But that's all ancient history now. I haven't seen Dad in 23 years. I haven't seen Bud in 24 I bet. But I've seen plenty of unholy, unkempt, unrighteous sons-of-a-bitches in that time to last me forever.

In 23 years, I've become a fairly decent shot with the Glock. I can't say I could hit anything more than 30 yards away, but when they're charging you with an axe (*my* axe, again) and you're 10, maybe 15 feet apart, well that ain't too hard for anyone I don't suppose.

But I'm getting ahead of myself. That's not how my story

e a lake

begins.

3 Days Before WOP

I was once, many years back, a logistics manager for a major chemical company. The name of the place is unimportant. The same goes for my job when I look back on it now.

Recalling the day it all fell to hell, I still grimace at my overreaction to the situation. I was tracking down a lost railcar full of caustic chemicals. My underlings were no help; the car had been missing for several weeks and our customer was screaming for results. Thus, it landed on my desk.

The nice lady with the soft southern voice on the other end of the phone reported her progress to me.

"Railcar DURX-89108 is in the Savannah, Georgia switching station," she said, her tone more confident than she deserved to be. "I can have it rerouted tomorrow and it should arrive in Dallas by the end of the week."

Closing my eyes, I began to hear my heart thumping against my eardrums.

"That's really nice, Ms. Bounden. However," I drew a deep breath to quell my anger. "I'm still looking for car number DURX-10893, not 89108."

The silence from the other end of the phone line drove me

nuts. I'm not even sure how my coffee mug ended up in my hand at that point.

"I'll have to do some more digging," she replied. I could hear the fear in her words. She'd screwed up. "I could have sworn that Peter said he was looking for DURX-89108. Are you sure that isn't the missing car?"

When the mug hit the wall of my tiny dark office, it exploded into hundreds of pieces. Coffee dripped down the wall like blood on bricks, just like you'd see in an old horror movie.

Within the hour, I was in front of the company president.

Before the end of the day, I was told to take a much needed two-week vacation. My job was causing too much stress, the president claimed. *No shit*, I thought, *What was your first clue? The 80-hour works weeks, the perm-a-bags beneath my eyes, or my salty disposition that got worse as the week went on?*

My wife couldn't get off on such short notice. And that was fortunate for her. I'm sure the last thing she wanted to do was to go north with me to an old cabin in the middle of nowhere and watch me decompress for 10 to 14 days. Her work as a nurse kept her busy enough. She didn't need my hassle, and I still don't blame her.

I was 25 at the time; Shelly was 24. No kids, two cats, and

talk of a dog. We had plenty of money, just no time. We both worked like fools so we could save as much as possible to afford kids someday. *Someday* isn't on the calendar, just so you're aware.

I almost skipped the cabin idea, but my wife got a hold of my dad who talked me into it. Hell, I hardly ever went there. It was an all-day drive from Joliet to the UP. It didn't make sense for a weekend jaunt. Drive there one day, enjoy a few hours, sleep, then drive back the next.

Dad reminded me of the exact directions. They weren't hard; drive north and when you hit Lake Superior, turn around and go south about an hour.

There were two towns equidistance from the cabin: Covington, population of about 500 (less, but that's fine), and Amasa, with about 350 calling that wide spot in the road home. I didn't need people. I needed quiet.

If I only knew then how much quiet I'd be getting. Well, would of, could of, should of.

2 Days Before WOP

There were no tearful goodbyes. Shelly had to run to a meeting that August morning, I needed to get the oil change on my dark blue 2005 Explorer, and I'd be back within a week or two.

So we exchanged a kiss, not all that passionate, and she played with my hair as she told me to relax and have fun.

Those were the last words my wife ever spoke to me.

The all-day trip took me exactly 10 hours after stopping for lunch in Fond Du Lac (that's in Wisconsin, in case you're wondering — at least it was back then). By eight in the evening, my vehicle slipped into the spot next to Dad's slice of heaven. And it was the exact dump I always remembered it to be.

The first thing I noticed was the amount of debris on the roof of the place. Small tree branches, a fair amount of leaves, and approximately 700 pine trees worth of pine needles decorated the brown log structure's top. Well, if Dad and Bud didn't find it crucial to clean that crap away, who was I to argue?

See, Dad and Bud use this mostly as their hunting and

fishing hideaway. My dad's dad originally purchased the land back in the 1930s, or maybe it was the 1940s. All I know is that in today's dollars (at least what the dollar was worth 23 years ago), it was nothing more than pocket change.

The upkeep is an annual project mostly taken care of in the late fall after most of the trees have shed their leaves. I was just early to the party this year. No bother to me; I wasn't going to take away any of their fall rituals.

It had been eight years since I last set foot on this property, or anywhere in Michigan's Upper Peninsula for that matter. Though I can't say that I had missed it, it did have a certain Henry David Thoreau type of appeal.

Until I stepped out of the vehicle.

Which was worse, at that time, I can't recall. Perhaps it was the swarms of evening misquotes out for the daily bloodletting. Maybe it was the bird-sized deer and black flies that circled my head, looking for an opening to inflict as much bodily harm as possible.

I know how to avoid both now, but back then I was a mere novice at such north wood's feats.

I flipped the power on, as per Dad's detailed instructions, and unloaded my truck as fast as I could. By sunset, maybe an hour after arrival, I was settled in with the sound of June bugs and millers pounding at the screens, downing my first bottle of expensive bourbon.

That was my simple plan. Week one: hole up in the cabin in an all-out blind, drunken pity party. Week two: sober up, figure out if I needed to change jobs, and plan my return to society.

That turned out to be a real horseshit plan, but it wasn't my fault.

One Day Before WOP

I think I remember most of my first night in the dank cabin, before the alcohol kicked in that is. The next morning, I awoke on the couch, naked and shivering from the chilly air trapped in a place with the world's worst ventilation. Drinking. Drinking a lot. That's what I remembered.

Being naked was no big deal. Bud told me he and his college cronies used to do it all the time back in the day. That was the advantage of being where, as he called this place, the rocks fall when people toss them to the middle of absolutely nowhere.

I did put clothes on that first morning. Well, old sweat pants and a stinky sweatshirt I found hanging by the door. Hitting the outhouse, I noticed most of the bugs had abated. A few mosquitoes did lazy loops around my head as I tried to relieve myself of all the toxins I'd ingested. Needed to make room for the next batch, beginning very shortly. I noticed a deer fly trying to find a spot to land. A wadded up magazine took care of that issue.

Eating a couple of granola bars, I waited for my water to warm on the old gas stove. I needed coffee badly. Perhaps that was one of my issues with stress and rage; I was over-caffeinated. I played with the radio but found nothing, unless you call static a victory. In that case, I found almost a million stations of loud, annoying static to listen to. Dad had always said if you wanted radio up here, nighttime was the best, and only, time to listen.

By noon, I couldn't read the clock on the wall, even though it had to be two feet wide. Sober, I could have read the time from a mile away. Drunk, not so much. I don't remember the afternoon or evening, though I wish I had.

I had no idea what was about to happen, how much my life would change. A truer statement is this: no one anywhere had any idea what was about to happen to them. And no one's life would ever be the same.

But drunk me, Bob Reiniger, hadn't a worry in the world.

Day 1 WOP

I awoke on day two (my second full day of solitude) to problems. Many problems.

Problem one: a raging headache. Perhaps I wasn't the professional drinker I had always considered myself. History would argue with that, but the pounding that began in my head the minute I opened my eyes said the contrary.

Many times I went to Cubs and Bears games with my friends and drank so much beer that a legend began. Two hours of tailgating before the game, followed by a beer an inning (or quarter with football), and by the end I'd easily consumed a 12-pack. Yet, I was the sober driver by the time we made our way home. Each and every time.

Apparently, bourbon had a different effect on my system. But in my system's defense, I wasn't used to half a bottle at a time. So that explained that.

I found some aspirin and tossed them down with the last of my glass of water from the kitchen counter. Problem one solved, or at least was on the way to being solved.

When I relieved my bulging bladder, I knew I needed to take in a lot more water. If dark urine is a sign of dehydration,

I can't imagine what maple syrup colored meant. Aside from drink more water.

When I threw open a tap on the kitchen sink, I discovered problem number two: low water pressure. It quickly became no water pressure. That meant the circuit had tripped on the pump. That meant another trip outside, this time to the back of the cabin.

Staring at the three-circuit box, I found nothing out of place. Just for good measure, I clicked each of the three off and then on again. Problem solved, or so I thought.

Still, no water came from the faucet. Just a few drips, nothing more. Within a minute, they quit. I tried the radio, even though I knew no stations would come in. The fact that no static came in bothered me a little at the time, thus I inspected the interior further.

Not one single light would come on. Any appliance plugged into the power grid was useless as well. Only the stove worked, and that was because it was run by LP (liquid propane). As for everything else…deader than Grant himself.

I took a hit from the open bourbon bottle on the end table next to the couch. Absentmindedly, I swished the brown liquor around my mouth, staring out the front window. Crap, I was going to have to get dressed, clean up a little, brush my teeth, and head into Covington. I needed to check with the Power Company when they thought they might get the electricity back up and running.

Fifteen minutes later, I emerged from my hiding, keys in hand, ready to run my single errand of the day. That's when I discovered problem three; and this was a biggie.

Day 1 - continued - WOP

My lips twitched, fingers fluttered slightly above the sticky steering wheel. While it may have been cooler in the cabin, the August morning outside was nowhere near as agreeable. The thin t-shirt I'd thrown on already had rivulets of sweat showing through.

Why, on God's green earth, was my Explorer dead? That was problem three. I must have left the dome light on following my hasty bug-forced retreat two nights back. But it was a weird scene that morning. The dome light, nothing. Twisting the key in the ignition, nothing. Not even that ever-present *bing bing bing* when you insert the key into the switch with the door still opened. Nothing.

Logic told me two things: the power was out in this remote area (not all that unusual from what I recalled) and I was an idiot for not checking my vehicle over before relaxing inside for two days. One was my fault; the other had nothing to do with me.

Heading back to the front screen door of the place, I paused, listening to the sounds of the woods. Birds still called, an assortment of small rodents, mostly squirrels I assumed, chattered here and there. Even the ever-present insects still swarmed about my body, searching for a convenient avenue to attach themselves.

It was peaceful, serene, quiet.

Considering that morning some years later, that should have been my first hint there was something different. It was quiet; too quiet. If I had paid attention, I would have noticed the absence of the sound of any car approaching. I would have noticed that the pulsing, low hum of the power-lines was missing. But I was a fool.

Back inside my humble and hopefully temporary dwelling, I sat on the couch, stunned by the morning's events. No electricity was explainable. This area was remote; hell, remote made it sound like a sleepy Chicago suburb. You know the type: soccer and dance moms hustling about on their morning walks, chatting about this and that. A number of fools much like me, grudgingly hopping into their low-mileage SUVs, off to work. Kids pounding a basketball into the driveway, occasionally tossing it up, hoping it would go through the hoop.

This was nothing like that.

If the wind blew from the north, you lost power. If the wind gusted at all from the east, even at night, radio stations refused to give up their locations. And when it rained, you were stuck inside a place that would eventually begin to smell like rotted wood.

My vehicle issue was easily explained away as well. I'd left something on and after 48 hours of sucking the life from the battery, everything was shot. But why wasn't I seeing any other vehicles pass by? There should have been a logging truck screaming past by now. Hell, 30 of them should have flown by, pretending the speed limit was for anyone but themselves.

But nothing; and that started to gnaw away at my mind.

Reaching for an opened bottle, I took a swig of liquor. Maybe that would help with my headache. Sure couldn't hurt, not at a time like this.

I resolved nothing that morning. Instead of investigating any of these odd occurrences, instead of making my way to the nearest neighbor (some five miles south), instead of clearing my head and even attempting to find logic where none seemed to exist, I laid on the couch, clutching the bottle next to my body.

And I drank until it all disappeared.

Day 3 WOP

Two days later, I found myself badly in need of a thorough cleaning. Somewhere in the middle of my drunkenness, I threw up on the couch, the floor and myself. I found my own body odor was offensive, so I knew it was pretty bad. And my teeth felt as if woolen covers lined them. That was all right, I suppose; the inside of my mouth seemed to have hosted the used underwear of a thousand Russian soldiers.

Except for the liquor, I wasn't prepared to be this alone for two weeks. While it helped pass the idle time, or what I could remember of it, day five told me it wasn't as good of a friend as I needed.

Still no power, nothing from the car either. Desperate for something positive, I pulled my cell phone out of my green canvas attaché and pushed the power button. I knew there wouldn't be a signal; I was too far from any tower for something that luxurious. But it would be nice to know the date and time, I thought.

Nothing. A formerly fully-charged cell phone failed to come back to life. Perhaps I'd left that on along with the light in my car. It was, after all, the only logical explanation.

I cleaned up again, using nearly all of the bottled water I had brought. Though I didn't know it at the time, it was a waste of clean water. Brushing my teeth over the kitchen sink, I watched a pair of grey squirrels play in a large oak tree behind the house. Whatever was going on hadn't affected their lives at all. Maybe I could learn something from them. Maybe I'd eat them, I joked to myself, if things got bad enough.

Walking down the edge of the blacktop highway, I kicked at the class-five on the shoulder. Small, light brown chunks of rock shot in every direction with each boot. I wondered how often they cleaned these remote highways. Back home, the street sweepers came by every month during the spring and summer. Did they brush these roads once a year? Or did they simply allow the snowplows, pushing mounds of white slushy snow aside, to do their work for them?

Four miles on a hot, sticky August afternoon is hell. Especially on foot. And especially when ten billion deer flies want to make you their bitch. I made a mental note to find a head-net or something similar for my next pilgrimage. If there *was* a next one. Hopefully the power would be back on soon and all of this could be written off as a bad dream.

As I strolled, closer to the actual highway at times, I

wondered what was going on back in Chicago at work. Were they even aware of the power outage some 400 miles away? Most likely not. This was a spot that not many in the office had ever heard of. Sure, some knew where the UP was, but only a handful had ever traveled north of Green Bay, and that was some 160 miles south of here.

Shelly popped into my mind suddenly. It was Sunday, maybe Monday — I wasn't sure. That either meant she was lounging on the three-season porch on the rear of the house, reading the Sunday paper, or she was hard at work. No matter where she was, she certainly wasn't sweltering in the August heat and humidity like I was. No, a constant stream of cool air surrounded her, whether in the car, or at work, or back home. She was lucky.

They say a man can walk at a rate of four miles per hour if he hustles. It seemed to me I was going slower than that. I knew I'd been walking for over two hours, and still I knew the house I was headed for was another mile down the road. I guess I wasn't really hustling. Hung-over meandering better described my gait.

By the time I reached the neighbor's front yard, and let's use that term *neighbor* loosely here, I was sun burnt, parched, tired, and had drunk the last of my bottled water. I hoped this was the only trip I'd be making like this.

The mailbox, which had seen better times, stated "Frank Morgan" lived there. Can't say I ever noticed that before, either as a child or the one time in the area as an adult. All I hoped for now was that Frank was home, friendly and generous with his cold water.

Day 4 WOP

"You're only the second person I seen in the past five days!" the old man squawked, sitting in a green, plaid recliner that had to be a few years older than him. And he looked ancient.

I sucked on my third glass of tepid water, finishing it and pouring myself a fresh one from the plastic jug. He said to drink it all, and I intended to drink.

"Say you're from Chicago, aye?" he shouted, pointing a wooden came at me. I figured he was almost deaf, given the volume he used.

I nodded, tossing back half a glass of water. I was almost feeling hydrated again. The sun really zapped it out of me. Well, that and the four-day bender.

"Yeah," I finally croaked. "Lived down there my whole life."

He scowled; probably didn't like "big city folk" too much. "I guess that makes you a Bears fan then."

I got a deep breath out and slid back on his pleather couch, which I imagined he must have salvaged from the local dump, during the Eisenhower administration, no doubt.

"You bet," I replied. "Love them Bears."

"That's too bad, that's too damn bad," he said, playing with the handle of his cane. "Most folks up here are Lions fans. Or Packers fans. Depending who's doing better in any given year." He shot me a crooked smile. "I guess that makes us mostly Packers fans then, since the Lions suck and have for a long time now."

Though I found Frank's conversation tantalizing, I had other needs to address still. Spotting an older cordless handset next his chair, I pointed.

"Do you mind if I use your phone, Mr. Morgan?" I asked in my most polite tone. "I really need to touch base with my wife."

He looked at me with indifference. Maybe he wanted money for the call. "Go ahead." He shrugged, laying his head back in his chair. "Wouldn't do you no good, though."

I paused mid-reach. "Why's that?"

He sighed and pushed his thick-lensed, black horn rim glasses high on his lined face.

"It don't work," he replied. "It hasn't in almost a week now."

I felt my heart begin to race. "Do you think something's wrong? Or perhaps you didn't pay your bill?"

When he smiled this time, I noticed his lack of teeth. There were one or two missing for every tooth present. It was kind of creepy, but went along with the theme of my visit.

"Oh, I paid my bill. Comes right out of my account on the fifth of every month." He tried to push out of his chair but only made it part way before giving up. "I was gonna show you my bank statement. Proves I paid it."

I rose and wandered through his cluttered living room. "Is your wife gone somewhere right now?" I asked, hoping she was.

"Oh, she's gone all right," he answered from behind. "Gone dead and shoved in the ground in the Methodist cemetery down in Amasa. So she won't be coming home anytime soon. Been dead 10 plus years now."

I turned and glanced at the old man. "I'm sorry." It seemed like the decent thing to say.

He looked at me with a strange face. "Why should you be sorry? You didn't kill her, did you?"

For a moment I froze, not sure how to respond. Soon the smile returned to his face and he laughed until he coughed. It was then he looked at me seriously.

"We need to talk," he said, all humor gone from moments before.

***

"You got a woman?" he asked in a direct tone.

"I've got a wife back in Chicago."

He shook the news away with the toss of his head. "How much you weigh?" he asked, changing directions.

"About 200, maybe 210."

"Muscle or fat?"

I had no idea where he was headed with this, or what his point was, but I played along. "I'd say half and half. I still hit the gym two or three times a week. But I drink a lot of beer on the weekends."

His face turned sour. "You're gonna want to give that up."

Okay, I had played along long enough. "What's your point, Mr. Morgan?"

Finally, he grinned. "Call me Frank."

"Okay, Frank; what are you getting at?"

"Sit down." He motioned for the couch. "This could take me a bit to get out."

Frank had me fetch him and myself a fresh glass of water — so much for sitting. Then with a thoughtful, almost nostalgic gaze, he began.

"A man came by yesterday, on his way from Covington, south to Amasa. You know where Covington is, right?" I nodded.

"So he claims he was up there when the power went out. Says no one has electricity, no cell phones, no landlines, and," he peeked over his glasses at me, "practically no running cars."

You know the feeling when your body freezes over? Where the hair on the back of your neck stands up straight? Yeah, that times two.

"A few older things run. Tractors, riding lawn mowers, some old motorcycles. But anything from the 80s 'til now is all dead."

To say I was skeptical would make it sound like I'd found everything Frank told me as gospel truth.

"How'd he get here?" I asked.

"Bicycle. Must have ridden right past your spot; surprised you didn't see him pass."

Well, that would have been impossible. Mostly because I was drunk. And passed out on the couch, probably in the middle of blowing chunks in my dreams.

"And that's not the worst of it," the old man mused.

My God, it got worse?

"Some lady up there has a short wave radio that still works," he continued. "According to her, the whole country is in the same shape."

Stroking an almost week's worth of beard, I wondered how much of this was true and what portion might be slightly exaggerated.

He coughed again and spit his phlegm into a wad of paper towel. "When I was a kid, we used to worry about nuclear war breaking out. The Russians would blow us to kingdom come, and we'd do the same to them. End of the world, we said."

"This sounds more like an EMP attack," I interrupted. Looking up at him, his face was more stock than mine. "That's Electromagnetic —"

"I know what it means, son. And it ain't good." He emphasized his point with a curt nod.

"No, it's not," I stammered, wondering if what he said was true.

"But it wasn't that," he whispered, pulling at his chin. "It wasn't no EMP attack on the U-S-of-A."

That confused me. Electricity, cars and phones not working…nationwide? It had all the earmarks of just that kind of attack. But now he claimed it wasn't. My stare begged for more from him.

"It's worldwide," he added quietly. "That gal told my friend it's the same in Canada, and Mexico, and South America, and Europe. Even Russia claims to be suffering the same ill-effects of whatever this is."

An idea sprang to mind. "Massive solar flares?"

He shrugged one last time. "Whatever it is, it ain't good."

Day 3 - continued - WOP

I made it back from Frank's quicker than the journey down had taken. Besides causing me great anxiety, he had a few nuggets of decent information for me. He had known my grandfather for years; even my dad was a casual acquaintance of his. And that meant he knew about the property surrounding my cabin.

Though I hadn't remembered it, there was a hand pump delivering water from the well on the north side of the house, just into the woods. Frank told me that my father, and most likely my brother, used the thing each year. Once in the spring and again in the fall when having the water on inside might lead to frozen pipes. And just so he was clear, frozen pipes meant burst pipes eventually.

Also, if I did some searching, I'd find a weapon or two that my dad liked to keep stored at the cabin. He told me some places to look, but I didn't pay that close of attention. I wasn't a gun guy, and could never picture myself using one against another human. While I might poke around in search of said weapons, I wasn't going to waste a lot of time doing so.

He also told me about the pit my grandfather had dug years

back. It was lined with cement with a treated board, covered by a tarp. I'd find it somewhere adjacent to the southwest corner of the place, just into the woods, he instructed.

In the hole, the pit, I'd find all types of hand tools. Tools that would come in handy if we were in this mess for a while. He claimed my grandfather had built a shed once upon a time, but it got broken into at least once a year. And being a frugal man, he was sick and tired of buying new implements for the cabin.

The most important tools I would find in the pit, Frank said, were two axes and a splitting maul. And if the power wasn't back on soon — and he added it wouldn't be — I needed to get at woodcutting, and soon.

The moment I saw the roofline of the old place, I sprinted to find the pump. If memory served me correctly, I had two gallons of extra water I'd brought along, and I had already polished off one. Further consideration told me I needed a liter of water a day to survive. At least, that's what I thought I'd heard once on one of those prepper shows.

I stared at the old wood stove that took up the center part of the living/dining/kitchen area. Aside from the bedroom next to this area, it was the only room in the cabin.

My grandfather was a short man; five foot four if I recall what my dad once told me. Even by 10 years old, I towered over the man. He seemed shorter. Days followed by years followed by decades of manual labor (I never did know what he did for work) caused him to be slightly hunch-backed. Add the hump to little natural height and you have yourself a mini-grandpa.

Because of his lack of size, the ceilings in the cabin were unnaturally low. At six-foot even, I cleared most spots by a mere six inches. The doorways were hell; I can't tell you how many times either Bud or myself damn near knocked ourselves unconscious heading outside when we were teens. Fortunately, there were only two of those to dodge — the bedroom and the main door.

The low ceiling, so my dad claimed, gave a homey impression of the place. To me, and Shelly the one time she visited the place, it looked like a gnome house stuck in the middle of the woods. Because my grandfather built most of this place himself, the roof never reached its skyward potential. If the pitch of a normal home's roof is, say, 30 or 40 degrees, the cabin's is a third of that. And it probably needed new shingles to boot.

The location of the cast-iron stove was central to the main

room. Easier to heat everything that way. Well, once upon a time that was true. When LP was added to the cabin back in the late 1970s, the wood stove became a relic of a day long gone by.

Day 4 WOP

I got right at the water issue the morning after my trip to Frank's. I had an opened bottle that required my attention that evening. And if the lack of power kept up, I had plenty of time coming up to work on further issues.

The rusty pump stood about four feet high, just into the woods where I remembered it from my youth. Though it didn't seem like something that would still be working, Frank told me that these devices never gave out. As long as you had water in the well, the pump would do its job.

Just be sure to prime it first, he warned, shoving a crooked finger at me. Prime is good and I should have water flowing within five minutes.

Acting like I knew what he meant, I nodded at his advice. If only I had asked what all was involved with priming such a device.

Thirty minutes of pumping only made my headache worse. Like it or not, I was going to have to slow down on the booze. That was okay; I only had four full bottles remaining. If this situation lasted longer than a week, and if I didn't slow down, I'd be out of booze quick.

Out of breath, I stepped back from the pump, sweat stinging my eyes. Wasn't priming just nice, slow, even strokes? Had I stroked the monster enough? Should something be coming out of the brown stained throat by now?

A little more pumping and I felt my anger rise. Not only was water absent from the scene, it didn't even sound like I was close to having it spit out anytime soon. I was missing something. But another humble walk back and forth to Frank's wasn't the answer.

Back inside the cabin, I contemplated the issue. No water from the pump yet, though Frank claimed it worked just fine. Dad and Bud used it three to four times a year, again without issue, as reported by Frank.

The problem had two sides.

First, and this was a possibility, Frank was full of shit. Let's face it, he was an old man, sitting around all day with nothing to do but wait for death. Maybe he didn't know any of my family. Maybe he'd never been to the cabin, except to sneak around and pilfer tools when no one was here.

But that didn't make sense. Frank knew right where the pump and well were. And he called my grandfather, father, and brother by name. If he was full of shit, I decided, it was only half-full.

The opposing side of the issue was me. Maybe I was doing something wrong. Either pumping too fast, or perhaps too slow. My knowledge of a hand pump was limited, as in pump the handle and water should come out.

My ignorance of this device as well as the rest of the cabin was far too great to write off as innocence. A strange world surrounded me, one that lacked the necessities and niceties that I was used to. If I ever wanted coffee and was too lazy to make it myself, I ran to the local coffee shop. Shelly was gone for the night? No problem. Dozens of restaurants sat within a few miles of my house. My car made a funny sound or wouldn't start? Call the auto shop.

My life was easy, almost cushy. My before, that is. In the cool, quiet cabin, I slowly came to the realization that I was unprepared for all of this…whatever *this* was.

Day 4 - continued - WOP

Standing in the doorway, I noticed something strange on the highway. Some 20 yards from my front door stood a woman. A middle-aged woman in a red sundress with large yellow flowers.

Stepping outside, she noticed me and smiled. Waving, she came closer, like a long-lost friend. Her blonde hair hung past her tanned shoulders, and as she came closer, I noticed her red sneakers. Though it was hot and the world was without power, she was dressed for success.

"Hello!" she shouted. "I'm so glad to find another human in this Godforsaken place."

I noticed the sheen of sweat on her face, pooling slightly on her upper lip. Yeah, she was not immune to the humidity either, regardless of how nicely she was dressed.

"I don't suppose," she continued, grasping my arms and squeezing. "I don't suppose I could bother you for a sip of water and maybe a small bite of food, could I?"

"You see, I took off from our cottage back down that road," she pointed to the south where many dirt roads intersected the main highway, "and I didn't realize how far it was to civilization. I guess I never paid that close of attention."

She waved a sweaty hand at me. "I'm Barb, by the way." Her smile was the best thing I'd seen in days.

"Bob Reiniger," I answered, shaking her petite hand. I pointed to the door. "Why don't you come inside and get out of the heat for a moment."

Her smile was white and quite something to behold. She even took my arm to follow along.

And that's when the lights went out…for me.

I came to just outside the cabin's front door. Peering up from the sandy dust, I noticed the door sitting ajar. But that wasn't the worst of it.

The back of my head ached terribly. Getting up on my hands and knees, I tried to shake off the grogginess. It was like waking up in the morning with a bad hangover, only I hadn't been drinking.

Flopping onto my butt, I spied a chunk of cut and quartered wood next to me. About a foot long and just the right size for someone to hold in their hand…and whack me across the back of my skull.

The last thing I remembered was a pair of boots next to my face. Brown, dirty men's boots. Not the dainty pair of red sneakers that were on Barb's feet. Nope, some male friend of hers had other plans, and it dawned on me that perhaps Barb did as well.

After crawling inside, things made a whole lot more sense to me. Gone was my attaché case, along with my laptop, cell phone, and several hundred dollars in cash. The door of my refrigerator sat open, the dark insides picked clean. That meant several blocks of cheese, some smoked sausage, and the rest of my water had left with the visitors as well.

For some reason, they left the bourbon. Perhaps it was because it was hidden in plain sight on a cardboard box next to the front door. Still, it surprised me they hadn't bothered to look. Maybe they were teetotaler thieves. Go figure.

I checked the cupboard next to the sink and found a sealed tin with graham crackers inside. They were pretty soft and mealy, but they might have been my only solid food left. Grabbing a fresh bottle of liquor, I cracked the lid and took a healthy swig.

Still getting my bearings, I sat on the couch until the bourbon kicked in. Every other swig, I'd take a bite of cracker.

"Well, this sucks," I said aloud, though no one was there to enjoy my misery.

The cracker and booze came up so quickly that I didn't

have time to make it to the sink. Catching my breath, I wiped my chin and stared at the new pile of puke that would need to be cleaned up.

"Yeah," I moaned, lying down on the couch, "this sucks big time."

Day 7 WOP

"You got robbed," the old woman said to me, between puffs of her menthol 100 cigarette. "You got to be careful up here, sweetie. There's a lot of unseemly folks that wander around this place."

Frank had told me, several days back, about another neighbor. This gal lived about three miles north of my cabin, just off the highway. Lettie Hamshire was a north woods lady through and through. Born in the house she still lived in, she had buried both parents somewhere on the property after their deaths. Never married, Frank claimed she was one of "those kinds" of gals. I knew what he meant, but doubted he knew much about the scenario.

She blew smoke in my face, waiting for me to speak.

"I figured that much," I replied, chasing away the flies that circled us in her garden. Why she chose to stand there in the hot sun was beyond me. Her opened, shaded garage was a mere 15 feet away.

"You need to be mindful of strangers," she continued, going back to her weeding.

Around us was one of the largest gardens I had ever seen. It had to be an acre, I surmised. Though I had nothing to gauge an acre against.

Beside us stood tall green tomato plants. To the left were some type of green beans, growing on poles and strings. Various types of squash and several watermelons sat further back in the garden. I had to admit, Lettie was quite the gardener.

She looked to be 60, maybe 65. Tan and fit, the only thing lacking was her height. She stood a strong head shorter than me, but had more energy than most people I knew half her age. Dirt and weeds became airborne as she tended to her patch.

"Do you know anything about hand pumps?" I asked, following her down the row.

"I use one every day for the garden," she replied, the almost used up butt hanging from her leathery lips. "Pump the handle up and down and water comes out. Pretty simple really."

"That's the problem. No matter how much I pump back at the cabin, water doesn't come out."

I studied the top of her sunbonnet as she lowered to pluck a weed by hand, one that must have been too close to use the tool. When she looked up, I noticed her short gray hair poking through several spots on the worn headdress.

"Did you prime it, plenty of water?" she asked.

I squinted at her. "Come again?"

"Did you pour a couple cups of water down the throat before you started pumping? You have to do that, otherwise you can pump from now 'til kingdom come and you won't get no water."

Ah, the missing step. But another problem.

"I…ah," I stammered, shifting from foot to foot. "I lost the rest of my clean water to those bandits a few days back. Can I borrow a jug from you?"

I had spent the last three days lying on my couch, drinking and feeling sorry for myself. Only a terrible thirst and large pangs of hunger had driven me from my spot this day.

"You can use river water to prime, sweetie. It won't affect the well at all. Hell, you could probably drink the river water up here. You might have a bad case of the trots for a week or so, but eventually you'd get used to it."

She paused her maniacal weeding, pulling her pack from her shirt pocket. I watched as her lips twisted, pulling one of two available death sticks out.

"Dang it all," she complained. "I think I only got one pack left in the house."

Big deal, lady, I thought. I didn't smoke. Not my problem.

"You're gonna have to be a dear and run up to Dizzy's for me tomorrow. Fetch a carton of menthols and tell him to put it on my tab. I'll get over there to pay him when the power comes back on."

Wiping the river of sweat from my chin, I peeked down at Lettie. Was I supposed to take her seriously? Did she somehow think one little nugget of advice on a pump equaled an all-day trip on my part to support her habit?

"And Dizzy's is in Covington?" I asked, hoping she'd notice my skepticism of the 20-mile journey for cigarettes.

"Oh heavens no," she cried, slapping my forearm. "He's just up the road a mile or two from your place. On that dirt road to the east, the first one."

"Does this road have a name?" Seemed like a decent question.

Her crooked gray smile displayed several missing teeth. Probably rotted out from too much tobacco.

"We just call it Dizzy Drive. You'll find his place about a mile back in there. Just after the crick crosses under the road. You tell him Lettie sent you and maybe he'll be friendly. Though sometimes he's a nasty man."

I headed back to the cabin with a small bag full of beans,

three cucumbers, four green tomatoes and a jar of preserved venison. Lettie also gave me instructions to arm myself. Maybe that would keep the burglars away.

"And don't forget my carton of menthols!" she shouted as I was about to lose sight of her home. "And bring them to me right away when you get them. One pack ain't gonna last me all that long, sweetie."

She was awfully generous with both advice and food. I guess that made up for her bossiness. Now, I had to find a place to hide my supplies. Then, I remembered the pit.

Day 9 WOP

It rained like a son-of-a-gun for the 36-hour period after I returned from Lettie's. Just before sunset, I heard the rolling thunder. Within an hour, rain was falling in sheets.

I thought about the old gal, watching the water pour off the front roof of the cabin. Maybe, likely, she was out of smokes. Though I had strict instructions, from a complete stranger mind you, to return the following day with her menthols, I knew she understood the weather. Add to that the sneaking suspicion she had a stash somewhere and my guilt never reached a critical level.

The road leading to Dizzy's place was muck and mud. The whole road. The ditches were filled with leftover rainwater and some of the sparse remaining gravel had been washed away in the low spots. It was a good thing I had three pairs of shoes with me; the boots on my feet were going to need to dry out in the returned sunshine and warmth.

Combating the nasty bugs was an issue I hadn't lived with in Joliet. There we had a mosquito patrol squad run by the city. The flies were only bad about two weeks of the year. If I set up a poop-slurry (don't ask) in the backyard, most nights were tolerable.

Here, in the precise middle of nowhere, the flies lived without worry of destruction. According to Frank, they only went away in the winter. Otherwise, they were just a fact of life. Having killed maybe a thousand in my first week, I realized that hadn't made a tiny dent in their population. Nor did the deaths of their family and friends quell their quest for blood.

It took almost an hour to hike back to Dizzy's place. Either Lettie sucked at distances or the mud had slowed me that much. I'd have plenty of time to consider that on my swatting walk back to my cabin.

The old rundown trailer that came into view as I rounded what I hoped was the last corner of my journey was nothing short of underwhelming. It was hard to believe anyone, even a man who went by Dizzy, lived in such a dilapidated place. The yellow siding was dulled from what could only have been years of neglect. I could see dull blue tarps lying across the roof, flapping in the warm breeze. Not one window looked clean. Perhaps the cleaning lady had skipped Dizzy's…for the past decade or so.

The collection of junk in his front yard was amazing. Old lawnmowers, both the walk-behind and riding variety, took up a large chunk of land nearest me. Behind them and to the rear of the "home" sat a half-dozen or so faded rotting trucks. All had their hoods lifted high. Most were missing any sort of window glass.

Rounding the trailer, I spotted a large pole barn that didn't have a door. It was just an open area full of more crap: washers, dryers, a cement mixer, what looked to be part of a satellite — all tossed about in a random pattern.

A fat bearded man came from the shed, wiping his hands on a rag. It was hard to tell which was dirtier, the rag or his hands. He spotted me, then reached and jerked a pistol from his rear pocket.

"Stop right there!" he shouted, waving the shiny metal gun at me. "I'll drill you right where you stand if you don't state your business instantly."

The thought of dying this far off the beaten path, in the middle of sheer madness, at the hands of a middle-aged wild man wasn't too tempting. I froze and raised my hands as instructed.

"Dizzy?" I asked, a quiver finding its way into my voice.

He shot me a mean glare, his eyes narrowed with suspicion.

"Who wants to know?" he barked, the gun still pointed at me.

"Lettie sent me," I replied, daring a step in his direction, seeing the recognition of his neighbor's name cross his face.

The gun lowered, not all the way, but it wasn't pointed at my body any more. "You with the IRS?" he demanded.

Another couple of steps and I felt brave enough to lower my arms. "God, no. I'm a neighbor. Bob Reiniger." I extended my hand before noting his weren't just dirty, they were full of grease.

"Reiniger?" he asked, shaking my hand with a firm grip. "Down my road and south on the highway?"

"One in the same." I was glad the standoff was over.

"I know your old man. And your brother shot a big buck practically on my front step a couple years back." He began to amble towards his dwelling. "Come on inside, I'll grab us a beer. Too damned hot to be standing out in the sun without something to drink."

Bravely I followed, wondering if the inside was any better than the outward appearance of this place. But I was hot, and beer sounded pretty good.

Day 9 - continued - WOP

Dizzy shoved some dirty clothes from a chair and pointed for me to sit. Meanwhile, he opened a stained blue cooler, pulling two beers from inside. Popping the tops on a kitchen counter edge, he handed one to me.

I expected it to be warm, almost as hot as the day. Instead, it was only tepid. Bonus points for Dizzy.

"I suppose you want to talk to me about raking your roof this winter," he began, leaning on the counter, casually paging through a nudie magazine. "Not sure I can do that this year. Not 'til my truck works again."

Okay, I was thoroughly confused. First off, why would he think I wanted to discuss snow removal on perhaps the hottest day of the year? Further, it seemed he was ignorant to what Frank had informed me had happened. If that weren't bad enough, why did he toss me another magazine from his two-foot stack on his counter? I couldn't imagine what disgusting things I might find inside, both printed on the page and of the more organic nature.

"Actually," I said, taking a slug of some of the nastiest brew I had ever tasted, "I'm here because Lettie needs another carton of cigarettes. Apparently you're her dealer."

His face screwed up something wild. "That old bitty still owes me for the last two," he raged, pounding his fist on the counter. I noticed dirty dishes leaped up and down with the anger. "Her credit ain't no good with me no more. You go tell her that."

Me? Did I look like the messenger service to this hillbilly? Add that to the fact that I had never met two people more willing to pawn their chores off on complete strangers.

"You can probably tell her that yourself." I gave him a half-smile and took another large gulp.

He shrugged, tossing the magazine aside. "Truck's broke down, so I can't."

Pausing for a moment, I wondered just how aware he was of the current situation we were facing.

"Power seems to be out, too," I offered.

That didn't seem to shock him. "Yeah, ain't paid my bill in a while so I imagine I need to run up to Covington to take care of that. Once it goes over $500 they get pretty serious about collections."

I scanned the hovel for a landline, but only noticed his cell phone lying on the counter. "Any luck with the cell?"

He shook his head, looking as defeated as a man could.

"Ran out of battery," he said, sighing before he flopped onto the laundry-coated couch. I assumed it was all dirty. "Can I get you to charge it at your place and run it back to me when it's done?"

I had to admit that for an outward ogre appearance, Dizzy had a charming side.

"I don't have power either," I answered, watching his eyes for any hint of recognition.

He nodded, peeking in my direction. "Didn't pay your bill either, aye?"

I felt a jolt of reality shoot through my body, starting in my head and racing for my extremities. He had no idea what was going on outside of Dizzyland. The world had ended, and he wrote it off as just his own bad luck.

Leaving Dizzy's, I brought home three cartons of cigarettes, three beers, and four large packages of venison chops from his defrosting freezer. The bonus was the mountain bike he gave me. Well, sort of gave me.

Even with the mud, the ride home took a quarter of the time the walk there had. Granted my back was covered in brown liquid goo where the rear tire kicked the rooster tail on me, but I felt renewed and refreshed. I even started formulating a plan. Emphasis on formulating, not plan.

Dizzy insisted I pay for everything he gave me, even Lettie's smokes. But I had little cash, only $35 in my wallet. With a laugh, he shook away my offer to let him keep one of my credit cards. Said he didn't believe in the things. My checkbook had been stolen with my attaché, so that was a bust as well.

His ingenious idea was to scribble out a list of all he gave me, assign prices to each item, and have me sign it — a sloppy type of IOU. Once the power came back, he expected a check or cash for the amount — $145. And within three days preferably. His last demand only solidified in my mind that he couldn't comprehend what was happening in the world outside of Dizzy Drive.

The smokes cost me, Lettie actually, $30 per carton. That seemed awfully low, even for a non-smoker. But I don't believe Dizzy had his thinking cap on tight when I was there. He wanted to give me the beer but I insisted on paying. Another $10 added to my IOU; again, fair.

We agreed the venison would be going bad sooner rather than later, so what he gave me was his gift. And with the present came with a promise that I could come back and get as much as I wanted. He admitted with a blushing face that he had almost three freezers full of the same. Something told me "hunting season" had its own definition to the humble woodsman.

He insisted on $45 for the mountain bike. Some yuppie, his words not mine, had a problem this past summer and couldn't get his bike attached to his Volvo properly. Rather than risking a scratched gold exterior, the young man left it with Dizzy saying he'd be back in mid-September for it. He wasn't coming back, I told Dizzy. Not this September, or next, or anytime in the foreseeable future.

Thus, a machine I knew cost $1,200 new, was placed in my care for $45. Best deal of the day.

Day 20 WOP

My plan for the future was simple, perhaps crazy, but straightforward. I was going to take my new expensive toy and pedal all the way back to Chicagoland. My plan wasn't short of critics though.

"You're gonna need a weapon," Frank warned my one chilly September morning. "I don't have an extra gun, just a nice compound my nephew leaves here. I think there's four dozen arrows to boot."

Thoughts of Daryl Dixon, the crossbow-wielding survivor, ran through my head. When I mentioned the name, Frank just stared back at me blankly. I guess he wasn't a "Walking Dead" fan.

"I don't think I need a weapon," I answered, taking a hit from the brandy bottle we passed back and forth. "I just need to get back to civilization, my wife."

He scratched his scraggly gray beard and stared out the front window. "You think a ham radio would work without electricity?" he asked.

"No, they need to be plugged into some type of power source."

His lips twitched for a few seconds. "You think that fellow I talked to back at the start of this was filling me full of hog manure maybe?"

The thought had never crossed my mind. But his words made sense. "Why do you suppose he'd do something like that?"

"If they had an old generator, one without all that newfangled circuitry, maybe they could get it to work," he added.

We were on two separate thought patterns. Two vehicles traveling the same direction, but on parallel highways.

Sitting quietly, passing the bottle back and forth, I noticed his eyes narrow. He nodded to himself several times.

"Radiation," he finally huffed out, almost sounding like he used his last breath to do so. But he was still alive; another swig of the cheap brandy proved it.

I opened my hands, confused.

"What about radiation?" I asked.

He shook his head. "Gonna be everywhere. That nephew of mine works for some nuclear company. Talks all the time about how close to Chernobyl we could be. Always claims if the power grid ever went down, we'd all be screwed."

I hadn't thought of that. I knew the Chicago area had several reactors. Most large metropolitan areas did. But something as bad as what happened back in the mid-1980s in Ukraine, that I doubted.

"Have to take my chances," I replied, feeling the effects of the liquor work through my mind. "I'd really like to get home."

Frank finally glanced back at me. "Don't blame you. Just that we don't have radiation up here."

He shrugged and went back to the bottle. "If you leave, be sure to stop by," he stated. "Spend the night. We'll drink up the rest of my stash and you can start out with a hangover. That'll make you think."

But I already was thinking. My plan needed refining.

Several days after my sobering visit with Frank, I pedaled up to Lettie's place. There I found her, resting in a chair in a small patch of shade. The cool weather of a few days prior had passed, leaving us sweltering in heat again.

A smoke in one hand and a glass of water in the other, Lettie saluted my arrival with the tip of her glass.

"Let me get you something to drink," she called out cheerfully. Moments later I too held a flowered Tom Collin's glass of water. She offered me a cigarette, which I waved off. There was no reason to start another bad habit at a time like this.

"Got a question for you, Lettie," I began, taking a large swig of the clear liquid. Instantly, fire filled my mouth and throat.

"What the hell is this stuff?" I coughed, sniffing the contents.

"Expensive Russian vodka," she answered with a chuckle. "I was saving it for when my time came to be with a man. But I decided today was as good a day as any to sip on it."

Trying to shake the caustic fumes from my head, I sat back in the green garden chair. Though the chair sat in the shade, the back was still warm against my sweaty shirt.

"Wow, good shit," I said, taking another smaller sip.

"You think you can get me another couple cartons from Dizzy?" she asked, tossing the spent butt into the gravel near her feet.

It was funny. Three weeks ago I had never even met these unique folks. And they all accepted me as is; albeit they saw me as their personal errand boy, but that was okay, too. "I'll see what I can do. I want to run my plan by you, see what you think."

"Leaving here is a bad idea," she said, looking my way. "Here is safe. Out there," she waved her loose-jointed arms before her, "is the unknown."

"I haven't even told you what I was going to do yet," I countered, playing with the tall tumbler of firewater.

"I got lots of time on my hands," she replied. "Nothing *but* time, and tending to my garden. Once I saw you on that fancy bike, I knew what you'd be thinking."

Day 22 WOP

I heard the *putt, putt, putt* of something coming down the road from the north and stopped in my tracks. Hauling brown water inside to boil on the stove could wait. I needed to make sure I wasn't dreaming and that the sound was an actual vehicle, of some sort, coming my way.

It was a vehicle all right. One that only a very unique person would use for travel. And it moved slower than anything I had ever seen on a highway.

Dizzy grinned broadly and waved, pulling the old Simplicity garden tractor right up next to me. With several sputters and one loud *pop!* at the end, the engine finally died.

"Damn thing runs!" he shouted, climbing off the seat.

"Does it go any faster?"

He laughed, slapping my shoulder with his dirty paw. "About the speed of spit is all it gets up to. But it beats walking my fat ass all the way down here."

He grabbed a satchel from the back of the tractor and handed it to me.

Surprised to receive a gift, I half expected a hand-written bill to follow. I cocked my head.

"What is it?"

"Venison," he stated, pulling a pack of smokes from his shirt pocket. "Figured you were running low, and I'm not sure it will keep much longer. Cook it right away, and cook the hell out of it."

For the last two weeks, my diet had consisted of venison, a few vegetables from Lettie's plot, several dozen cans of pork and beans from Frank, and lots more venison.

I never had much of a taste for deer growing up. Too gamey for me, especially the deer from this area. Absent any decent farm crops, the wild things mostly ate browse. Pine cones, twigs, green weeds, everything that tasted like the ground it came from. And I decided with the first pack from Dizzy, that ground must have been spoiled up here.

"I've been cooking the hell out of most of it," I answered, leading Dizzy inside my cabin. "Still tastes the same. If I had seasoning I could maybe improve the palatability of the stuff."

Dizzy looked at me funny. "Isn't there anything in the pantry?"

I shook my head at his strange words. "What pantry? There's no pantry here. None that I've found at least."

He pointed north, towards my bedroom. "In the closet, in there."

"Show me," I demanded.

Shrugging me off as likely the stupidest man he'd ever met, Dizzy trudged into the bedroom and tossed aside the curtain covering the small offset opening. There, on the left end, he removed a panel. Peering into the dark area, he smiled.

"You got all kinds of shit in here," he exclaimed. "Grab me a flashlight and I'll show you."

I didn't have a flashlight, so a candle had to do. Staring at the small yet stuffed area, I felt my jaw loosen for the first time in weeks. Utopia.

Dizzy and I emptied the contents of the pantry onto my bed as I took inventory.

12 cans of Spam

6 cans of cocktail wieners

4 boxes of mac and cheese

3 massive cans of pork and beans

2 jars of mayo

1 gallon of cooking oil

Various spices, nine containers

4 sealed boxes of matches

18 tall candles

2 flashlights, no extra batteries

2 cases of shotgun shells

4 boxes of handgun shells

9 mm Glock

Lifting one of the cans of wieners, Dizzy studied the label, licking his lips as he did.

"Man, I love these things," he whispered as if having a food fantasy right there in my bedroom. "Can I have one?"

I pointed to the pile. "You can have all six," I declared, watching this face light up. Those were my least favorite food in the world. One time, back when I was maybe 12 or 13, I got sick on an overnight camping trip with the neighbor kid and his dad.

The only reason I had gone to the camp-out was because Timmy Glassner had said his mom was coming. And I had one huge crush on that woman. She didn't come, and his dad brought the cocktail wieners to cook over the fire. Somewhere in the middle of the night, they all made a mass exodus through my throat.

Dizzy laughed openly at my idea of leaving. He found no logic in my plan.

"You don't know these people up here like I do," he said, already enjoying his second can of delightful miniature wieners. It wasn't so much the meat that grossed me out, it was whatever was in the sauce that made my stomach do flips.

"And I'll bet ya a hundred bucks it will take you a month to get there...if you ever do," he added, licking the remaining juice from his fingers. My stomach did a back flip noticing how greasy his hands still were.

"It's about 400 miles, Dizzy. If I average as little as five miles an hour, that's 80 hours. Pedal 10 hours a day, I'm home in 8 days." I could see the doubt in his eyes still; there was something he wasn't sharing.

"The first guy who sees you on that bike will try and take it away from you," he replied, wiping his hands on my bedspread. "Eventually, someone will probably kill you for the bike and whatever supplies you take with. And what you gonna do for water? You need a gallon a day, ya know."

The water didn't worry me. The news of someone wanting to kill me for the bike was rather disturbing. I pressed him for more information.

"There was this guy, Al Acorn," he began. "I know, funny name. Anyways, Al lived up on the way to Covington. He had a thing for gals. As far as I knew, he kept it under control...

except when he drank. And he drank a lot."

I didn't like where this was headed, but I nodded to keep the story moving.

"So some people up there, some backwoods hicks, decided to have a talk with Al. One day he's around, the next he wasn't." His eyes stared at the patterned bedspread as he recalled the incident from some years back. "Rumor is they took him out in the woods and slit his throat open. No more trouble from Al after that."

My ears began to ring, contemplating rumors and ghost stories recalled by a man who probably hadn't seen the inside of a school building since eighth grade, if that. I wondered how much was true. And I wondered what his ulterior motive was, if any.

"You don't want to get yourself killed over something as stupid as a bike, Bill."

I shook my head. "Bob."

He looked at me with a stupid expression. "Who's Bob?"

"I am. Bob Reiniger. Me."

"I thought your name was Bill!" he exclaimed, rising from the bed, pulling his pants up somewhere near his sizable waist.

"Nope, it's Bob." I had no idea where he got Bill from.

He shook the mistake away. "Whatever. I just think you'd be

better off staying here. We're friends now, and friends don't let friends make dumb choices."

Dumb choice or not, my mind was made up.

Day 26 WOP

I spent the next few days preparing for my trip. I had a few changes of clothes that I washed, as best as I could without soap, by hand. I ate extra meals, making sure I put the maximum amount of protein I could into my body, which meant venison. I even loaded up with extra water; drinking a glassful every time I passed the clear bottle I left on the counter.

The pump worked, eventually, and I had plenty of water. But I still felt the need to boil it in large batches on the two-burner stove in the small kitchen. Though it remained stained with the impediments from the ground, I knew I was killing most of the bacteria that might try to do the same to me.

Lettie gave me a backpack one of her nieces had left behind. I wasn't crazy about the pink color, but I needed something to carry supplies in. And it was a sturdy, if not rather effeminate, carrier.

One afternoon, Dizzy showed me how to load and fire the handgun we found in the closet. I didn't want to use it ever, but he convinced me it was the safe bet. Even if I only fired over people's heads, they'd get the idea rather quick that I was armed and ready to use force.

The morning I decided to leave was a cool one. A thick fog blanketed the area, giving my surroundings a mystical look. Aside from a few blue jays calling for one another in the woods, the only sound for miles was the gravel crunching beneath my tires.

Taking one last peek at the cabin that had been my home for almost a month, I mounted the bike and headed down the road. Eight days would lead me to Chicago: home. I wondered about the look of shock and surprise on my wife's face. Would she have stories like I'd have? Was Chicago suffering like this area, and if so, was she safe? Or was this an isolated incident, caused by some device from the cold war, stored in a remote northern Michigan location?

Only time would tell. Eight days of time.

I was just settling into a good rhythm when the loud *pop!* broke my concentration. At first, I wasn't sure what it was. Perhaps a rock shot from under my tire and struck something in the woods. Or maybe an animal had stepped on a dead branch nearby alerting me and all of the woodland critters of its presence.

The front of the bike started to wobble. Leaning forward, I

searched for the problem. Trouble struck then, and it struck hard.

One second I was pedaling away, minding my own business. The next, I found myself lying on the blacktop, unsure of what had just happened.

The bike was three or four feet behind me. I tried to shake away the blow to my head when it met the black highway at approximately five miles an hour. Touching my scalp, I touched the sore spot and noticed the crimson stain on my fingertips.

I lay back, right in the middle of the highway nearly on top of the faded yellow stripe that divided the two lanes. It wasn't like someone was going to come tearing down the road and run me over. In all my time here, the only working vehicle that had passed by was Dizzy's dippy garden tractor.

Taking a few minutes to gather my wits, I finally rose and inspected my ride. As suspected, the front tire was flat. Something had caused it to blow. I wondered if that "something" had been planted by my fat friend. Quickly I shook away that thought. If anything, Dizzy was harmless.

Striding away from the crash site, I set my jaw, and mind, on my continued journey. If I couldn't ride home, I'd walk.

It took all of 100 yards before the pain in my back and

right ankle convinced me to stop. Apparently, the fall had been more severe than I first thought. Checking inside my pant leg, I found the cause of the pain. An ugly stripe of road rash covered my right calf. Further investigation showed my ankle was bleeding, badly.

I hurled the backpack as far as I could towards the woods in disgust.

"Damn it all to hell!" I screamed at the top of my lungs. A faint echo seconded my feeling.

I wasn't going anywhere. Not anytime soon at least.

Day 36 WOP

I don't know how many days I laid on the couch, taking sips from the latest bourbon casualty. If I couldn't be traveling, I may as well be drunk.

Night after night I rested, listening to the eerie howls from nearby coyotes. If I had had the strength, I would have joined them. But the sound of their cries reminded me what a wild place this was.

Dizzy was delighted to find me back home, if I dared call it home. Treating my wounds, he showed me a compassionate side I didn't know existed. Making a large pot of venison stew was his way of bringing a casserole.

Using what was left of his almost rancid meat and frying it to an almost black hunk of leather, Dizzy added it to a pot with a small amount of water. Already in the water, boiling the life out of them, were a dozen or so small potatoes Lettie had given me several weeks back. For a finishing touch, he added a small amount of flour to thicken the sauce.

It tasted like shit, but it was edible.

"You're lucky the wolves didn't get you," Dizzy pontificated on one of his daily visits. I had always suspected he'd come back the first day to pilfer what he could from my remaining stock. Discovering his friend had returned, he only borrowed two cans of Spam .

Rubbing my forehead, I laughed at him. "There's no wolves here, Dizzy. I know that much. You're not frightening me that easily."

When I looked back, he seemed serious. "There's wolves here," he added dryly. "They've moved in the past 10 years, from over in northern Wisconsin."

"Wolves?"

He laughed. "Hell yeah. And you gotta be careful starting now through spring. Those bastards will follow you everywhere. And if you get in trouble, they'll eat you."

Oh, good God. Wasn't it bad enough I was stuck in the middle of nowhere? Without power, or communication, or a vehicle? Now I had to worry about carnivorous neighbors too?

This place really sucked.

"I brought you a roof rake," he stated as if telling me he'd brought me a shirt.

"Don't you need it?" I asked, knowing that when the snows came, his flat roof was far more susceptible to collapse.

"I got four," he replied, nearly bragging. "So I figure I give you one, you can keep up with the snow."

I nodded, rising from my slumber spot to fetch a spoonful of nearly black nourishment. "How often do I need to clean the roof? Once a month or so?"

It was his turn to gawk at me like I was the idiot in the room.

"Try every time we get more than six inches or so," he retorted more sarcastically than I'd ever heard.

That made sense. My roof had virtually no slope either. "What's that, like three or four times a winter up here?" I asked, slurping a large chuck of burnt venison from a spoon.

"Try a lot more than that, Bob. Last year we got eight feet of snow." His eyes flashed in my direction, showing me his wisdom. "Now that's more than normal. But we should get at least five feet this year. That would be normal."

Depression set in. I needed to cut some wood, but my injuries had kept me pretty much bedridden. Well, that and the blind drunken rampage I'd been on. But that would be short-lived. I only had a bottle and a half left to enjoy.

Every time I cut wood, to prevent myself from becoming a human popsicle that winter, I'd have to be on the lookout for man's best friend of the not-so-kind and friendly variety.

I wasn't getting home before winter. I would simply have to

wait for spring. If I lived that long.

Day 42 WOP

Killing a man, when you're desperate to stay alive, is nowhere near as hard as the average person might believe. I understood the "kill or be killed" mentality my cousin, a United States Marine, mentioned to me several times. And putting that in action was simpler than I'd ever imagined.

I heard him before I ever saw him. The intruder kicked open my front door; it was unlocked so that was unnecessary, and stormed into the cabin screaming at the top of his lungs.

It took him a minute in the dim candlelight to figure out where I was. That was the break I needed. It gave me a chance to get my bearings, enough to figure out what the hell was going on in the middle of the night.

He charged at me. I saw the glint of steel in his right hand. Cocked above his shoulder, the knife hurtled at me in the dark. I rolled away to miss the stab, ending up on the cold floor on the far side of my bed. He readjusted his attack, but that's when I warned him to stop.

Dizzy had convinced me trouble would be coming, eventually. I had to get used to sleeping with the Glock near me in bed, preferably under the opposite pillow. A place where I could reach it as needed.

The wild man fell across the bed, stabbing at me in the dark, missing. But he was way too close. I knew I couldn't get around the bed, past him, and out into the larger area without taking a poke from the blade. I racked the upper receiver on my pistol.

"Hold it right there!" I screamed, waving the gun so he could see I was armed. I wanted, *needed*, to give him every chance possible to retreat. At that point, I still had no idea why I was being attacked.

"Ahhhhh!" he screamed louder, thrusting at me again and again. He wasn't going down without a fight. That much was obvious.

I fired a shot a foot or so over his head into the ceiling. The gun roared louder inside than I had anticipated. Instantly my ears rang. He continued his fight, unfazed by the gun.

"I'm going to kill you!" he shouted, lunging again, shoving the knife where I was. Luckily, I moved in anticipation of his desperate swing.

"Leave, damn it!" I shouted, whacking at his body with the butt of the black pistol. Maybe if I could inflict enough injury to the menace, he would get the idea I was serious.

He crawled across the bed with the speed and agility of a

spider. Another swing of the blade came close, too close. He caught the outside edge of my left shoulder as I tried to crawl deeper into the closet.

Rising again, I saw his silhouette against the poorly lit doorframe. The blade rose again as he drew nearer. Instinctively, I fired at his center mass, just as Dizzy had told me to. Not once, not twice, but six times. I'm sure the last three or four shots zipped over his prostrate body, now flat on my former sleeping spot.

Shaking so badly I almost couldn't hold the gun, I poked at his motionless head. No response. I shoved the barrel into his shoulder, and nothing came from the man.

Backing further into the closet, getting as tight into the far corner as I could, I listened and only heard my ragged breathing. Shaking intensified as I tried to draw a deep breath. The smell of gunpowder filled the room. The sound of my sobs soon followed.

Day 44 WOP

If my calculations were correct, it was somewhere around October 1st. I guess it didn't really matter, not at that point. Whether I killed a man on September 30th or October 3rd was inconsequential. The deed was done; kill or be killed. I appreciated my cousin's sage-like words more now. He was right; a man's will to survive is stronger than even himself dares to believe.

At daybreak the morning after the attack, I was still huddled in the closet. The barrel of the gun, my gun, was still pointed at the man's head. Though I knew he was dead, I was against taking any further chances.

By the time I braved rising from my spot and scurrying around the body, the sun was high in the sky. The old battery-powered clock on the far kitchen wall showed it was 10:30. I'm not sure I slept more than three hours. Dead men may tell no tales, but a sneak attack — hours in the planning — wasn't going to be my demise.

I boiled some water and threw in the grounds Lettie had given me in the gallon size can. Though I wanted a drink, coffee seemed more sensible at that point. My ears still rang from the half-dozen or so shots I'd fired in the small room. That only made the pounding headache worse. Hopefully, coffee would help.

Standing in the doorway between the rest of the cabin and my bedroom, I studied the man. Well, the mortal form of the man. His soul had departed this wretched Earth a number of hours earlier. His clothes were dirty and stunk of body odor. From what I could see of his left hand, he was no cleaner than Dizzy on any given day.

I thought about turning him over, maybe moving him out into the yard. But I thought better of it and decided to go get help after coffee.

I hope Dizzy had some cigarettes left. This was the day to start another bad habit; to hell with healthy living.

Dizzy came back with me right away. He even gave me a lift on his putt putt, as we now called it. With no muffler to soften the sound, it was loud. My headache couldn't have gotten any worse, that just wasn't possible.

"He's dead all right," Dizzy confirmed, poking at the body. "Deader than a polecat flattened in the middle of the road."

Dead was dead, thus, no such thing as deader. But I kept my thoughts to myself.

"Any idea who he is?" I asked, not willing to touch the body myself quite yet.

"Let's turn him over and find out," Dizzy replied with more than a tinge of excitement. A game of identify the stiff. Oh, yay!

I let Dizzy do the rolling, and any required body touching. Once upon a time, when I was eight, I saw my dad touch my dead grandmother in her coffin. I was shocked and appalled he would actually reach in and touch a dead person. I get it now; it was his mom and he wanted one last touch from the woman he loved so dearly. That day I made a promise to myself; I was never touching a dead person.

I had to look away from the scene when he rolled the corpse over; the urge to vomit hovered near the extreme level. Half the bed was stained a dark crimson.

"Whoa," Dizzy exclaimed loudly. "That's a lot of blood. I bet you nailed this sucker in his heart."

"Do you know him?" I asked, still facing the wall.

I heard him smack his lips several times, apparently Dizzy's way of filling the silence as he thought.

"Can't say I do," he replied, his voice trailing off. I turned slightly to see what he was up to now. "What do you say we pull his shirt up and check out where you hit him?"

"God! No!" This guy was crazier than my attacker. "I want nothing to do with a dead body."

Dizzy peeked at me from the corner of his eye. "Well, we need to move him so you can use your bed again. You and I need to drag him out into the brush."

I shook away both suggestions. "I won't be sleeping in this bed ever again," I answered. "And just why are we going to drag him out into the brush? Shouldn't we dig a hole first?"

He laughed at me. Dizzy laughed out loud at me as he sat down next to the dead guy on my bed.

"He tried to kill you," he informed me. "He don't deserve to get buried. We'll drag him deep into the swamp out back. Maybe a mile or so. Let the wolves and coyotes pick his bones clean."

My stomach turned again at the thought of an animal ripping the flesh off my dead bones.

"That's a little barbaric, Dizzy. Even for you."

He shrugged my doubt away. "We ain't gonna waste a good hole on this piss-ant. Come on, grab an arm."

Day 45 WOP

I stared at the dead man's driver's license, taken from the wallet found in his back pocket by my less-than-sensitive friend. John Adams. Huh. I thought he'd died years ago, the same day as Thomas Jefferson.

Mr. Adams, allegedly from Ironwood, Michigan (if you can trust the DMV) looked no better in the picture on the plastic card than he had on his deathbed — maybe *my* death bed — or bed of death.

According to Dizzy, Ironwood was over 100 miles to the east and slightly north. Mister Adams could have walked here in the days since the world ended, but why? Or was the address listed on his license simply of the "last known" variety?

My larger concern was how many more John Adams' were out there, desperate for what little I had? And when was the next one coming?

The prevailing theory followed the logic of a madman. Adams was hungry, or thirsty, or lost. No one knew how long he had been wandering the highways of the desolate land. His last meal could have been the previous night, or two weeks ago. Hunger, Dizzy and I deduced, was the only thing that drove him to the dark place where he wanted to kill me for what I had.

Water wasn't really an issue up here in the UP. At every turn, a person like me could find a stream or river or lake that held decent enough water for human consumption. It was the most plentiful resource this place offered.

Shelter was another thing in good supply. Though dozens of summer cottages dotted this area, all but four were occupied now. Dizzy thought it wise that I go scavenge what I could from the empty abodes, but I was hesitant. Killing the wanderer made me cautious, wanting to hide in my cabin with gun in hand all day. Longer jaunts were going to have to wait.

One thing that was harder to come by now was food. Dizzy's supply of ill-gotten venison was gone, either eaten or rotted. True, he had a shed with stacks of supplies, but he said that would only get him through the winter. Lettie had a basement full of goodies and was more than willing to share.

Frank had enough for himself, he claimed. He didn't eat much, didn't do much, didn't need much, or so he said. He would be happy if I ran him a jar or two or Lettie's preserved wild game a month. Bear or deer, made no difference to him.

As best as I could figure our little group, albeit spread over 10 miles, had enough food for the winter. Even into spring we'd be fed, Lettie claimed. Water wouldn't be an issue. When it became too cold to run to the pump, I was told I could just take a bucket and scoop up the plentiful snow that would be as deep as my head. Just let it melt inside and I'd have all I needed for the winter.

The one thing I was lacking was a massive woodpile. Since the only heat the cabin offered had to come from the wood stove, I'd need a lot of the stuff to survive the long, cold season. Lettie and Frank each had four cords, delivered this past mid-summer by a guy from north of Covington. Even Dizzy had a pile that was 40 feet in circumference and six feet high.

I could have all the wood from Dizzy, but it needed to be hauled. He agreed to come and help me cut a bunch before the snows came. It was a nice offer, especially from a man I wouldn't have given a damn about two months prior.

But how hard could it be to cut a bunch of wood for myself? I had the tools and the time.

Day 50 WOP

The gun roared in my hand and the animal in front of us trotted off as if I were no threat at all. She had that right. It was the ninth deer I'd missed in three days. And this one was a mere 30 yards from us.

"You have to be the worst shot I've ever met," Dizzy laughed, watching the doe bound through the brush. "Here I bring you to my secret spot, set you up with an easy shot, and you still blow it."

I had no words to defend myself. Fourteen shots at nine deer, mostly standing and broadside had resulted in no harm. Unless you count my ego. That was taking a battering.

Though I'd spent three years in these woods with my father and brother, I had never taken a deer during that time. I was never too interested in killing anything, so I shot maybe once or twice. My father just shook his head at me mostly; Bud laughed each time I touched one off and had nothing to show for the shot.

Now Dizzy took the spot of both. Chastising me for ruining his prime spots and finding humor in my misfortune. Easy for him, he had taken a fat doe two days back. He and I were eating pretty damned good, for the moment.

Trudging through the sunlit forest, I pulled the collar of my coat a little tighter to my neck. Gone were the warm days of late summer, where a long-sleeved shirt was all you needed. Fall came early in these parts, I knew that, but Dizzy liked to remind me.

"See that sugar maple over there?" he asked, guiding me easily through a maze of brush and bogs. "It was crimson the other day. Now it's turning blood red. All the birch have gone from yellow to dead already. And the wooly caterpillars are everywhere."

Keeping pace behind him, I waited for his lesson. Surely he wasn't just playing John Muir for me.

"And?" I prompted. "What does this all mean?"

"Gonna be a long, hard winter," he answered, slowing down to weave in and out of some pines branches. "You'd best be ready."

He was just trying to piss me off, I figured. Give me a hard time about my woodpile again, or lack of woodpile in my case.

"You know that shit isn't so easy to chop by hand. I've been at it for almost a week, and my pile has grown." Defending myself was hard; I wasn't really all that interested in manual labor that made me feel as exhausted as chopping wood did.

He stopped and turned, shoving a finger into my chest. "Winter is coming."

Waiting for a grin, I noticed him poke me again. "All right, Eddard Stark. I get it."

His face turned confused. "Who's he?" Dizzy asked.

"You don't watch much TV, do you Dizzy?" What a dumb question. Nowhere did I see a satellite dish on his property. Cable wires? No, just a few power lines. And the nearest television station was over 100 miles away. Except for a fat-tubed color set, the oldest VCR known to mankind, and a stack of skin flicks (as he lovingly called them) that would have made Ron Jeremy proud, Dizzy had no need for such a frivolity.

"You either need to get two cords cut, or figure out how to haul that much from my place," he continued. "And I'm out of gas, so the putt putt ain't gonna work no more."

Leaning against the trunk of a large oak, I thought about his advice. I needed venison and wood. Dizzy would happily supply both, but I felt I needed to be able to produce something myself as well.

"I'm gonna head back to my place," I told Dizzy, seeing his trailer in the distance. "I still got a few hours of daylight. First thing I'm going to do is drag all those chunks out of the woods on the west side. All that stuff my dad cut last spring."

"Last summer," Dizzy interjected. "And that's good because it will be dry enough to burn this winter." He slapped my back, damn near knocking me over. This guy wasn't losing any strength in the dark days of the world. No sir, Dizzy was in his element.

Almost back to the highway, I paused to watch bright yellow leaves drop from the birch tree lining the road. Dizzy was right; fall had come quick and brief. That could only mean winter's early arrival. Marvelous.

My brother and father drug their hunting stuff back and forth each fall. Neither wanted to leave much at the cabin over the winter, afraid someone would break in and take their belongings. As such, I didn't have a winter coat or a decent pair of boots. Certainly not what Dizzy called winter boots.

Frank's feet were too small, as were Dizzy's. Anything they had would be three sizes tighter than preferred. And, according to both experienced woodsmen, tight boots got cold fast.

Lettie offered me a pair she had lying around. They were only a single size too small. Thus, they might fit the need.

Except of course they were pink. Not hers, she claimed. Just something some relative had left behind years back.

So I had a pair of boots that would work in a pinch, but what I really needed to do was scavenge around the area. Who knew, I just might find something my size, and a bit more manly.

Dizzy promised to dig through his back shed and find me a parka that would last the winter. Claiming to have clothes dating back to the 40s, he couldn't guarantee any coat he found would be fashionable — just warm.

A few more strides and I was on the highway leading home. That's when I saw it. Standing there on the shoulder, chewing on the last of the green weeds of the season.

The doe was small but vulnerable. Perhaps she'd never seen a human before. It was, after all, possible in these parts. My dad had said once that if a hunter went deep enough into the woods and swamps of this area, you'd set foot on land where man had never trod.

Slowly, trying not to spook the brown animal, I raised the gun. When the explosion sounded, the doe took off for the far side of the road.

Damn it!

Day 50 - continued - WOP

My heart fell when the tiny doe began her dash for the east side of the road. Fifteen shots and ten deer and I was zero-for-10. There had to be a worse hunter than me somewhere in the world. At least I hoped there was.

When I heard the crash just into the woods to my left, I craned my neck to see if the confused animal was coming back. Maybe she'd be closer, and dumber. A second chance at a (hopefully) non-moving target.

A thrashing sound came next. One that made me wonder if I was about to meet my first wolf. Then it died away, slowly, suddenly halting. I stepped into the ditch to investigate.

The first thing I noticed was blood at my feet, on a path the deer had taken in her hasty retreat. There were some on the road, I noticed. Not a lot, but enough to give me hope. And in the ditch just before the tree line, I found more, much more.

Bright red foamy droplets covered the ground near my feet. According to what Dizzy had said, that was a good sign. A double-lunger, as he called it.

Excitement took over once I was inside the forest. There, maybe ten feet in front of me laid the doe on her side, not moving. I noticed the gun tremble as I extended it at the animal, making sure it didn't jump up suddenly and sprint further into the woods.

By the time I reached it, I knew it was dead. Well, I was pretty sure it was dead. With each step, dead leaves and small twigs cracked under my dirty boots. And with each sound, the deer remaining motionless. So either it was a good faker, or she was dead.

I nudged her hindquarter with the toe of my boot — no response. Slowly, I circled towards her head, my gun still pointed at the deer. Gently I gave her one last nudge, just under her jaw.

She was dead. I was a hunter.

Kneeling beside the kill, I slapped its back quarter several times. Perhaps not as much meat as I might need for a month, but still something. And I had taken it. No one helped me.

"I can do this," I whispered aloud, smoothing the fur on the side of *my* deer. "I can survive this. I can make it to next spring. Then maybe, I can get home."

Rising up, I threw my arms in the air above my head. Pumping several times like Rocky Balboa celebrating his stair climb, I let out a small *whoop*. Remembering there was no one to hear me, I doubted Dizzy would have even heard the gunshots two miles back in, I shouted as loud as I could.

"Yes! Yes! Yes!" echoed through the otherwise silent woods. Only the pines, and maples, and birches partook in my celebration.

When the adrenaline quit pumping through my veins and my heart rate slowed to below 500, I studied my kill. It was double-lunged, just where I was aiming…I think. Dizzy claimed I only pointed the gun; "You need to aim!" was his typical battle cry after a miss. Well, aim this, sucker.

A problem came to mind, studying the deer. What was I supposed to do next?

My plan had always been to have Dizzy guide me through the next steps. He was the experienced hunter. Certainly more experienced than I was. But he was two-plus miles away. Most likely memorizing his magazines.

"Gut it," I said aloud as if I knew what that meant. I remembered that much from my limited hunting experience.

And that was a problem. I had never actually watched a deer's entrails being removed. Typically, I showed up an hour after Dad or Bud had taken and properly cleaned their kill. Even then, the nearby gut piles made me want to puke.

To gut this thing, my first kill, I was going to need a knife.

That meant running back to the cabin, finding a sharp knife, and making my way through the rest of the mysterious process.

I rose, glancing one more time at my deer. My deer. That sounded awesome for some reason to me.

Day 50 - continued - WOP

I ran most of the few hundred yards back to the cabin. Trotted was probably a better description. Though I was "fit," I wasn't that physically active in my former life. My exercise program included a weekly walk with Shelly, usually taken on Sunday mornings.

My wife had always warned me I needed more physical activity. "Some day you'll thank me for riding your butt," she often said. Usually, I laughed her off. But at that moment, I remembered just how right she was. Eerily correct.

Sucking in air, I scanned my small home. Somewhere someone must have left a decent knife here. A quick check of the kitchen offered one possibility. An old wood-handle meat knife with an edge duller than the lip of a wood table. If needed, I could make it work.

I lit a candle to dig in the deep recesses of the dark closet. Nothing. Did Dad really cart his hunting knives back and forth to Milwaukee every deer season? Didn't he know that I might be in need of one someday? Like when the world ended and I found myself stranded here, in the middle of nowhere?

I took a spot on the couch; my heart rate settled. There had to be a real-life hunting knife, somewhere, in a real-life hunting cabin. But where?

A thought finally came to me. Standing, I made my way back into the bedroom. Pulling open a dresser drawer, then a second, I spotted what I knew I'd find: Grandpa's old hunting knife.

My first recollection of the tool was my first deer season, some 10 years earlier. Grandpa, dressed from head to toe in woolen blaze orange, strapping a thick leather belt around his rotund mid-section. The only reason for the belt was to hold his knife, sheathed in a dark tan leather holder.

Back then, it and he were the coolest things I'd ever seen.

"Don't you dare touch that," he warned me at the time. "It's sharper than a surgeon's scalpel."

Grandpa died the winter after that deer season. Since then, the knife had sat in the same spot in the white painted dresser. It was my dad's homage to his dad. We all knew it was there; and that meant Grandpa was still with us, no matter what.

Picking the antique up, another voice sounded in my head.

"Don't touch that." It was Dad. I looked around the room, expecting him to be standing there. "That's Grandpa's knife. It belongs right where he left it. You'll just lose it somewhere. Grandpa deserves more respect than that from you."

I pulled the blade from its sheath. What I expected to find was a shiny steel knife with an edge that could slice on sight. However, I discovered something else.

A layer of rust covered the tool. And I mean the whole thing. Only the cracked leather handle wasn't covered by the orange coating.

"You two are such morons," I replied to the ghosts of my father and brother.

I needed to clean this thing up so I could gut that deer, hopefully sometime today.

I used a generous coating of cooking oil and a dirty rag to work on the rust. Happy with the results, I searched for something to tackle the last problem.

This knife was duller than my first find. While I was excited to get back to my kill and clean it, I knew I needed an edge that would cut something other than water.

Fortunately, someone had left a sharpening steel here at the cabin. At home, I did a lot of cooking, well actually more like the prep work. Shelly did most of the actual cooking. But I knew how to slice and dice. And that began with a sharp knife.

Drawing the metal against metal, I felt the dull edge give up some of its coating. This wasn't going to be a quick job, but with each pass I knew the knife was getting closer to being useful. And how sharp did it need to be?

My dad always claimed that a hunter's knife needed to be so sharp that he was scared of it. Well, this wasn't going to be that sharp. This would eventually end up somewhere between scared and concerned. Probably more on the concerned end of the spectrum.

The entire time I ran the blade down the steel, I tried to recall the process of cleaning a deer. I knew the guts needed to come out, that much was common knowledge. Even if I messed it up, which I would undoubtedly do, I couldn't make that much of a mess, could I?

After poking a hole just below the sternum, the next slice went up the rib cage. And I had to be careful to stick to the cartilage. Slicing through ribs would take the edge off the blade.

I was a little fuzzy on how to cut around the hindquarters. That was going to be an issue. But I shrugged it away, testing the blade on a piece of scratch paper I'd found. Perfect; I was ready.

The pelvic bone ran across my mind. I did a quick scan of the room. An axe would come in handy. Seeing none, I decided to play it by feel. I'd figure out a way once I was inside the bloody mess.

Day 50 - continued - WOP

I stood over the gut pile, winded. Sprinting back to my kill, I'd almost tripped twice. I guess I was anxious to get at this...the process.

But staring down at where my deer had been, the only thing left was a mess of blood and entrails. The deer itself, the one I knew I had killed a half hour ago, was gone.

I squeezed my eyes tightly shut before letting out a low guttural moan. Someone had swiped my deer.

Hustling back to the road, I first looked left, then right. Left — south — was nothing but a gloomy empty road. To my right, I spied a single soul, trotting down the middle of the blacktop. And if I was seeing things correctly, he had something slung over his shoulders and around his neck. Something large. Something that looked similar to a small deer.

It took a few minutes of running, something I wasn't really good at, to catch up to the man. Well, I assumed it was a man. Twice he had looked back and picked up his pace. Each time I saw his face and swore he had a beard.

"Where you going with my deer?" I shouted ahead when I

was within 50 yards of him.

He slowed and then stopped. Turning, I noticed his grin.

"This is my deer," he answered in a friendly way.

Yeah, that wasn't gonna happen. I stepped within 20 feet of him, winded but ready for action.

"My deer that I killed back there, just off the road," I continued, studying my thief. He was a little shorter than me, but otherwise we could have been kin, I thought. We both had longish sweaty hair, each had a scruffy beard, and neither of our clothing could be called anything but filthy.

"I have to warn you," he stated, laying the deer on the road. It was then I noticed the fresh blood running down the front of his tan leather jacket. "I have a knife. So before you think about anything goofy, just be warned."

I shook him off. Pulling the Glock from my pocket, I held it at my side.

His confident expression changed to one of guilt. "Huh," he said, his eyes moving from the gun to my face. "Guess you got me beat."

"I just shot that thing," I said, pointing at the deer. "What gives you the right to come take it?"

He shrugged first and then scratched at his face with a bloody hand. "Heard you shoot, came to see what was happening, and saw you run away from the woods, back towards that cabin on the other side of the road. When I came and checked, there was the deer."

"And it didn't dawn on you I was coming back?"

He laughed, wiping blood on his pants. "Me and my family ain't had much to eat in a week now." He pointed north, behind him. "We're camped up on the edge of the lake, about a half-mile in from the road. Safer that way. I was out foraging, heard you shoot, saw the deer. Well, you know how desperate things have become."

To be honest, he looked more ragged than I did. And I did understand his desperation.

"How many in your family?" I asked.

He held up four fingers. "Me, the wife, young daughter, and son. We had to leave Covington last week. Things have gotten a little unruly up there. Not safe for a family right now."

I wished it had just been him. That would have made it easier to chase him off. But a wife and two kids? Chased from their home?

"Make you a deal," I said, stepping between him and the deer. "You can have a front quarter."

The disappointment in his eyes was obvious. "How about a half?" he begged. "I did clean it after all."

How about nothing, ran through my mind. But that wasn't very neighborly of me and I knew it. If not for the generosity of my three new friends, I might have already been dead myself.

I let him cut one of the back quarters away. Ten minutes later he headed north, a deer leg and ham hoisted over his shoulder, and I carried the remainder back towards my place.

A thought kept running through my mind: What if he didn't have a family? What if he was just some road bum looking for a free lunch?

I made up my mind to investigate the lake and his cozy sounding setup. Not today, but sometime in the near future.

Day 65 WOP

Frank praised me for my generosity when I saw him next. People needed to help one another at a time like this, he claimed. Turning on your fellow man wasn't the way to act.

A few days after that, Lettie affirmed what Frank had said. She even gave me a hug, and a hearty one at that. I'd never taken the old gal to be much of a feeling person. Goes to show everyone can surprise you.

Lettie canned a good amount of the meat for me in glass jars. I dropped it off one morning and picked it up three nights later. Packed in each glass jar was a good amount of venison, half an onion (cut into smaller pieces) and one smashed bulb of garlic.

I dragged sixteen one-pound jars back to my place in a pull-behind carrier that was usually used to haul deer from the woods. Something my father and Bud *did* manage to leave behind that was of use to me. I figured that if I could make each container last three days, I had enough meat for a month.

Added on that were the dozen or so containers Lettie had given me earlier. Two months down; at least two more months of winter to cover, she warned.

Dizzy had agreed that the deer, taken a little more than a week back, was mine and I needed to tell that bum to pound sand. Winter was going to be tough enough without sharing with strangers. But it still made me think, weren't we all strangers a mere few months back?

I helped Lettie harvest the last of her garden just as the first snows arrived. As best as I could tell it was late October, third week maybe. Snow in Chicago sometimes came in late November, but typically later than that. But watching the small white flakes dot the back of Lettie's dark blue barn coat reminded me where I was. And that was most certainly not Chicago.

Dragging the final bag of potatoes down to her small, smelly root cellar, I searched in the near darkness for the jar she said I would find down there. Turns out, they were easy to find. Hundreds and hundreds of mason jars lined the far wall, in a way that made grabbing them easy.

"We're gonna need more lids come spring," Lettie said as I hauled 20 or so into her kitchen. There, over a wood stove, she prepared the last of the early spuds for canning.

"And where do we find those?" I asked, slightly winded

from all the steps.

She smiled as she began to clean the dusty clear jars. "Covington. And we're gonna need a big bag of salt, too. Fifty pounds I suppose."

I stared at her from a chair on the opposite side of the stove. "And you have money for this? Cause I sure don't."

"You and Tom will have to get busy killing deer," she replied, more interested in her canning than the conversation.

"Who's Tom?"

"Dizzy," she answered, sounding like I was a fool for not knowing that.

I had always wondered what his actual name was. It just hadn't come up in conversation yet. And I really wasn't much of a conversationalist when it came down to it.

"Tom Dizzienski," she answered as if I had asked for his full name. "We just always called him Dizzy. Like his dad was called."

"What'd you do for a living, Lettie? Before you retired?" As long as new info was abounding, this seemed like a good time for more questions.

"I worked at one of those nudie clubs up in Iron River," she answered, a sly grin rising on her lips.

"What'd you do there?"

I saw her roll her eyes at me. "I was a dancer," she answered with a slight giggle in her words. "That was years ago. But I made a lot of money in the 12 years I worked up there."

Now it was my turn to laugh. "I would have never guessed."

She glanced at me, still working on her jars. "I'm surprised Frank hadn't told you already. He was one of my regulars. When he wasn't out on Superior on a ship."

"You ever marry?"

She shook her head, pausing for a moment. "Never had much of a need for a regular man," she answered, scratching at some dirt on one of the containers. "Been so long now that I'm not sure what I'd do with someone else here, stepping all over my feet, getting in the way."

Outside, I noticed the snow picking up. "I should head back." I had a number of items in my cart and it was going to be slow going. Besides, daylight was dwindling and I didn't want to be out after dark. I wasn't ready for that yet.

"With the snow, there'll be more trouble," Lettie warned. "People will be getting desperate. You need to watch the road and around your place well."

Stories were beginning to abound of weary travelers,

desperate for food and shelter, breaking into occupied cabins and trying to roust the current owners. Sometimes they were fought off, other times things didn't end so well. But the increase of people on the highway brought tales of these escapades and the vermin themselves.

"You keep safe, too," I called back to Lettie, pulling my coat back on.

Her head tipped towards the corner of the kitchen. "My 30-30 is in fine working order," she replied, packing white potatoes into jars. "I just touch a shot or two off anytime someone approaches, and trouble avoids me." She shot me a peek. "You do the same now. Don't trust no one."

Those words and the thought of someone kicking me out of my warm cabin into the cold winter surrounding gave me food for thought on the five-mile journey home.

Day 65 - continued - WOP

Hauling my goodies back from Lettie's, I passed the lake. I had yet to try my hand at fishing, though I had discovered rods and tackle in a cramped corner of the bedroom back home. Maybe next spring I'd have a hankering for fish.

I paused at the road leading west along the north shore of the narrow lake. Down this road, I'd discover the man who had tried to steal my deer, along with his family. Or so legend had it. In the two weeks that had passed since our encounter, I had wondered about his story many times.

Most likely, he was a single man, making his way from one town to another. There'd been a number of men like that in the past few weeks. All seemingly trying to get somewhere before winter came.

He'd been lucky and stumbled across my fresh kill. He probably watched me in action and swooped in for the taking when the time was right.

Hunger causes a man, or women or child, to do things they wouldn't normally think of. I got it, I understood it, but I sure as hell didn't like it.

The snow had let up; just a few spits of white balls now and then. I was going to take that road to the west, go back a half-mile or so, and find this camp. Maybe I'd even discover his family, just as promised.

Leaving my cart behind, I felt the gravel crunch beneath my pink boots. Something told me I wasn't going to find anything at the end of this road. Perhaps a deserted place or two, maybe even an old used up camp spot where the man had squatted, enjoying my kill.

But I needed to find out if I was as big as sucker as I believed.

As far as I could tell, the smoke wafting into the heavy air came from a small fishing shack about 100 yards to my west. A set of three similar low-roofed dwellings sat in a row: one red, one yellow and one light blue. The blue shack had smoke coming from the chimney.

I supposed that some family owned all three. And just to make their cheery lives a little brighter, one of them came up with the idea of painting each similar hut a different color.

'Bradley and Mel's is yellow, Kim and Chuck's is red, and mine and Trevor's is blue. Isn't that just darling?' The voice of a thirty-something housewife rocked my mind as I inched closer to the drive leading to them.

There was someone here, but that didn't mean it was the man I'd met. And even if it was him, there was no guarantee of a family. I wondered how his face would show the shame when I realized I had busted his lie in half?

I noticed movement nearer the lake so I circled wide, not wanting to spook anyone. As I stepped closer, the man looked up. I knew it was the same fellow; there was still blood on his jacket, though a little darker and obviously dried by now.

The moment he saw me, I noticed his smile. He waved. "Welcome," he called out, lowering his wheelbarrow full of sticks and twigs to the ground. He came right to me and shook my hand.

"I wondered if you'd poke your head in on us," he continued, already dragging me towards the shack. "Nice to see a familiar and generous face again. You gotta meet the wife; she'll be dying to thank you."

It felt funny letting my guard down so quickly. One minute I was approaching, crouched in the brush, hand on my weapon. Now I was being brought inside for cookies and coffee.

"Marge!" he shouted as I felt the warmth rush out the opened door. "We have a visitor. Come meet mister…" He paused, looking funny at me. "You know, I don't think we ever introduced ourselves. I'm Warren Luke."

"Bob," I answered, staring at the small but homey interior. The insides were as blue as the outside, if not a little brighter. Two children appeared from another room. A girl I'd guess in her young teens, and boy no older than eight.

From the same room entered his wife, Marge. She did not possess the same look of amusement as her children. They may have been happy to meet some stranger Dad drug in off the road, but not her.

"Warren," she said in a low tone. "Are you sure this is safe?" Her eyes studied me as if I were Charles Manson himself. I noticed her nervous hands clutching at her apron.

He pulled me forward further into the warm room. "This is the man who gave us the deer two weeks ago," he stated in a boastful tone.

Her eyes opened wide, flooded by an honest smile. "Oh!" she exclaimed, rushing to hug me. "Thank you so much, sir. We were so hungry and down to nothing. You saved us." The children moved closer.

I wasn't comfortable being deemed their savior. For the most part, I gave up the hindquarter grudgingly. But they made it seem as if the messiah himself had just stepped into the room. I half expected someone to offer to wash my feet.

"You have on pink boots," the young daughter said, eyeing them with a grin.

"I'm not from here," I admitted, finally escaping their embrace. "I'm from Chicago. I just got stuck here when things went down." I peeked at her smiling face. "And you got purple hair." Her smile broadened.

"Do guys wear pink boots in Chicago?" the boy asked. I couldn't tell if he was sincere or making fun of my unique winter footwear. I went with the former.

"I was unprepared," I stated, being led to a chair by the man I now knew as Warren. Little did I know that I was unprepared for the news they had for me.

Day 65 - continued - WOP

They were from Covington, just up the road some 10 miles. Warren, Marge, Violet and Nathan — who preferred to be called Nate. Warren and his wife never offered their ages, but I took them to be in their 40s. Violet announced her thirteenth birthday would arrive with the first day of spring. I joked that might be a while off, maybe even June. The whole family laughed.

Nate would be eight any day now. But that was the problem. None of us knew what day it was anymore. I knew we were just over 60 days into this mess, whatever it was. Back at the cabin, I'd been keeping a daily journal of weather and game observations.

It struck me and my new friends as funny how in 60 days we'd lost touch and given up with most of the trappings of our former world. Cell phones, dead; internet, gone; running vehicles, almost nonexistent. Not only did it not matter what day of the week it was, it no longer mattered the date on the calendar. Or the time on the wall (they still had a working wind-up clock, though it may have been off by an hour or two).

Their story went, as mostly told by Warren with a few tidbits added by his wife, that they were sound asleep all safe in their home when things went quiet. The first few days passed without incident. But as with any panic, times worsened quickly.

By day four, or five if Marge was to be believed, most of the food for sale in Covington was snatched up. Hoarding kicked in quickly. That left the haves and have-nots. The sheriff and the mayor worked diligently to provide for all, but storm clouds hovered on the horizon.

"Somewhere after three weeks in, a group showed up on foot," Warren continued, his face pained as his sad story progressed. "They were armed pretty well, handguns and shotguns mostly. They damn near drank the place dry. When things started getting out of hand — like looting and robbing — the sheriff tried to step in. They shot him dead in the one bar on Main Street."

The air in the cabin cooled as Marge wrung her thin hands, pacing behind her husband. She picked up the tale. "The mayor went to ask them to leave. They strung him up just outside of town, on a pole that goes across the road stating, 'Welcome to Covington.' They said if anyone cut him down, they would kill the person."

I contemplated the ugly, unruly scene. "Didn't anyone take up arms against them?" I asked. "Fight force with force?"

"People were pretty scared at that point," Warren admitted. "No one really wanted to die. I guess we weren't that desperate yet. But when they kicked people out of their own homes and tossed them out in the street, the whole thing seemed hopeless. The consensus was to just let them take what they wanted and hope they moved on."

"Then about a month ago," Marge continued, "they started going house to house, taking whatever food and guns they could. We never had any weapons. Wish we had now." She took a spot next to her husband, neither looking into the other's eyes.

"We left in the middle of the night shortly after that," Warren stated. "Packed up as much as we could in four backpacks, two suitcases and a rolling cart Marge used for gardening. We knew these places were down here. Figured no one would have taken them yet."

The children hung near their respective parents, Violet on her mother's shoulders, young Nate on his father's lap. They had the faces of lost people; scenes I had only ever witnessed in pictures from wars. But they weren't some far-off foreign-speaking family. They were my neighbors, and this was our country…or what was left of it.

Day 100 WOP

Three feet of snow covered the landscape outside my drafty, but warm, home. I'd used Dizzy's roof rake nine times already since the snow started in earnest. I wondered if there were nine or 90 more rakings needed for the season.

As best I could tell, it was Christmas time. My adventure began in mid-August when the power went out of everything. My tally said it was three months and ten days later — or thereabouts.

For dinner, I allowed myself an extra ration of stew. Venison boiled in water, a touch of flour, carrots, beets and potatoes for extra nutrients. It wasn't my idea. Dizzy was the one who handed over his recipe happily.

Along with his cooking secrets, he allowed me to steal 50 bottles of the sacred brew he hoarded. Dizzy was a lot more resourceful than he appeared. His sheds held stockpiles of canned foods, bags of dried fruits and vegetables, and a fair amount of candy. In his back bedroom, never used for sleeping, he stored beer and water…mostly beer.

If I said he had a pallet of the brown liquor, I might be underestimating. Fifty bottles didn't put a dent in his stash.

And he invited me back whenever the weather allowed for 50 more, but that wasn't happening anytime soon. Not in this weather.

Allowing myself to think of Shelly back in Joliet, tears stung my eyes. Three Christmas' together and now one apart. I always thought that when the lights went out, she'd headed for her parents', some five miles across town. I hoped she hadn't waited too long. No doubt, the Chicago area got dicier than here, and much faster.

If she were lucky, and at home with Mom and Dad, she was most likely safe. But that was something I'd have to wait another five to six months to find out for myself. Fall's attempt to get home had ended in disaster. Any type of effort in the winter was strictly out of the question.

My beautiful pink boots, while warm, were two sizes too small when I donned enough socks to keep my feet warm. If I only wore one pair, the bitter cold nipped at my toes within minutes of being outside. The downside of that was my feet sweat faster and two pairs of socks were too tight and allowed for no circulation. End result: cold feet, again.

One warm jacket was all I took from Dizzy before the snows came. As long as I kept it dry, that was fine. And since I spent the majority of my time inside, tending to the fire and stew, I was okay with just one outer garment.

I had enough food, and water — as promised — lie everywhere just outside my door. Two things I was short on and either could kill me: company and wood.

To say a man goes stir-crazy without companionship after 30 days is like saying a person needs air every few seconds. It's just a given.

I'd spent years either in school, at work or hanging out with my buddies watching some game. My solitude mostly consisted of three partial deer seasons. At most, that meant six hours of silence for two days per year.

Even here in No Where (yes, that's the official name I'd given this place, I had a lot of free time to come up with it) I hadn't gone a week without speaking to another human being. Then the snow began. And like any good gift, it just kept on giving.

When it wasn't snowing, it was blowing. A 10-inch dusting, as Dizzy calls a snowfall that minor, pretty much shut you in. Twenty inches? Get the roof rake out. You can practically hear the roof trusses bending. Snows stops and you're fine? Hardly.

The snow abating meant the wind was ready to pick up.

And not some minor 10- to 15-mile-an-hour breeze. We're talking winds that shook every window in my ever-diminishing abode. With each passing day stuck inside, the walls seemed to inch in. And when the wind gusted up over 40 miles an hour, the walls hardly slowed it down.

Usually late in the night, I'd hear the wind abate. And that's not good. That meant cool, crisp Canadian air had settled in.

One morning, I arose and found the actual air temperature to be minus 35. That's 35 below zero. Even a roaring fire would hardly warm my hovel at that point. But there was good news about the cold; it didn't usually last too long. Just a day or two.

And then the snows returned.

Day 101 WOP

Wood was quickly becoming an issue. Most of the cut wood still lay at the back of the cabin. For some reason, I thought it was convenient enough back there. Oh sure, I hauled a couple dozen armloads to the front side and another two or three inside when the first heavy snow hit. But the bulk of my supply was out the front door and 50 feet around in back.

Ordinarily this wouldn't have been an issue. I could just slip on my coat and a pair of boots and fetch wood as I needed it. Winter made it a problem, though.

Aside from the 10-foot drift that blocked my front door one morning, I discovered something even more disturbing. The south and north ends of the cabin liked to buffer the winds just enough to allow snow to pile up on the corners. And not small piles.

The southern route had a drift that reached past the top of the roof — a good 20 feet — and extended another 50 feet out into the formerly open yard. The northern drift was twice as bad and made me depressed just thinking of it.

As such, hauling wood became an all-day ordeal. That was after two days of unburying it from another massive, well-packed drift of winter fun.

Another problem came to me just before Christmas. My woodpile was dwindling faster than I had anticipated. As much as I wanted to wade through the snow to go tell Dizzy he had been correct, I decided to use my waning energy and gumption to split more wood. At least while it wasn't snowing, or blowing, or 40 below zero.

That had been one day in the past month.

Given the amount of snow resting on top of my ready to use wood, it was hard to judge exactly how much I had left. But I knew there wasn't a whole lot left buried under the remaining snow. That left me with two possibilities.

First, I could cut more wood. I had been bright enough before the snow began to pile up to bring the axe and maul in the cabin. That would save me a whole lot of digging out back if I could even find the pit my grandpa had made.

On the other hand, I could just burn less wood. Up to that point, I had kept the fire in the small wood burner going at a fairly decent clip. I figured if I was going to be alone in the woods all winter, I needed to at least be comfortable. But now I saw the error of my ways and began cutting back.

However, I still needed to cut more wood. And for that, I needed a break in the weather. Watching another storm whip up the white scene outside my cabin, I knew that cutting was several days off, at best.

Day 112 WOP

I waited almost two weeks for the storm to abate. Well, first the snow, then the wind, and finally the cold.

Tools in hand, I made my way outside. The temperature wasn't as bad as I had expected. After I unburied the old-fashioned thermometer and let it adjust to the air, it read a balmy 18 degrees – above zero. Bonus!

It doesn't take much movement to warm up when you have on half the clothes you own. Within minutes, I had my jacket open, stocking cap tipped back, and could work for a while without my gloves.

Piling four 12-inch sections of chainsawed oak before me, I lifted the axe. The *thump* from the first swing sent shivers into my hands and up my arms. It was as if trying to split concrete instead of wood. Shaking away the pain, I drew the axe again.

With that thrust, I noticed a small fracture in the wood. The sound of the oak splitting cut the otherwise still morning air like a gunshot. A few more pounds and I had several smaller pieces of wood separated from the main stump. Progress was slow and painful, but still moving forward.

It took no time to work up a good sweat. I knew I hadn't

been at it for an hour, yet my coat, gloves and hat all sat on the bench near the front door. I may have needed them at first, but they'd become unnecessary options.

I ran out of energy quickly, far too quickly. My meager sustenance of stew and rationed water left me lethargic and dehydrated. My water intake had to be low. The effects of dehydration hit me with a dizzy spell and I took a short break to drink some water and catch my breath.

Who knew chopping wood was such hard work? I never had, though I also had never so much as lifted an axe before my forced confinement in the north. If some fashionable gym down in Chicago really wanted the latest trend that worked every major muscle group, I had a program for them.

By late in the afternoon, I had split enough wood to last a day, I figured. If memory served me correctly, and I was still a little light-headed, I burned between 12 and 15 hunks of oak each and every day. I had 12; 13 if you counted the one piece that was almost split into two smaller ones, so that was fairly close. I was going to have to do better tomorrow.

Eating my dinner by candlelight and the glow from the open stove door, I read an old hunting magazine between bites of stew. This batch was getting old; it had been on the stove three days. Lettie warned me, "Three days, then toss." It was ready for the toss pile.

According to what I read in a magazine from the 70s, people liked to eat bear. Some said it made the best stew meat around. Others claimed it was only good for stew, nothing else. I had only tried it once up there.

Dizzy had given me some freshly killed black bear meat for a change of pace one night. To be honest, it stunk my place up. I mean, worse than the usual gamey smell that followed me around. The meat was almost sweet but so greasy. I wondered if we ate different bear than they did back in the 70s? This couldn't be what they were talking about when they mentioned "a delightful alternative to venison," was it?

Thinking more on smells, I wondered how bad I stunk. Bathing didn't happen on a regular basis before the snow made it impossible to dive into a pond and clean up a little. Since the snow? I had maybe cleaned up once or twice a month, and that was being generous.

I lay back on the couch, my sore muscles screaming at me never to chop wood again. As I drifted off, I felt the aches in my hands, still quivering from the vibrations the axe handle delivered.

'*Don't do it again!*' my body called out. '*Just give up and give in;*

you're not going to make it anyway.'

I shook the temptation away. I *had* to make it. I was *going* to make it. I would not give up without a fight. The dreams started before I was in a full sleep. And yes, I dreamt of chopping wood, all night long.

Day 121 WOP

A good rhythm was all I needed. Suddenly woodcutting wasn't all that bad. My problem at first was the belief that I had to chop all I could in one session. I learned quickly that wasn't a good idea.

I started each morning with a hearty breakfast, stuffing as much fuel into my body as possible for the day's work. Along with food, I drank six cups of water, sometimes more but never less. I dressed in lighter layers. As long as the temperature stayed above zero, the sweat I worked up kept me warm enough.

I would chop wood from the existing stock of stumps until I felt it in my back. That signaled break time. A few more glasses of water and some jerky Dizzy gave me had me ready for the next step.

Little by little, an armload at a time, I hauled the wood from the back of the cabin to the front. Stacking it in orderly crisscross piles, I found more wood than I believed I had. After that, I chopped a little more and drank more water.

After a midday break, I began stacking my newly cut wood. Though it was dry enough to burn, it still didn't burn well enough to be the only source of heat. That meant a separate pile where I pulled one log for every four of older dried wood. That recipe would allow me to extend my heating season by another month or so, once I had the ready-to-chop wood processed.

After five days of that process, I stood in my front yard, still covered in snow, smiling at my progress. In the fall, when I was blind drunk, I could have never imagined adapting to my stark environment. The piles of light-colored oak told a different story now. They signaled a man who was ready for anything…almost anything.

One morning, in the middle of my trips around the cabin, moving wood, a figure approached from the road. Dressed in proper attire for a winter's day, the man (I assumed it was a man) wore crude wooden snowshoes to make his travel easier.

I noticed the grin, then the face mask fell away.

"What the hell are you doing out?" I asked, shocked to see Dizzy. As far as I knew, he was still holed up for the season.

He laughed, slapping his mitt covered hands together. "I needed some fresh air," he replied more optimistically than I expected. "I've been going out for a little bit every day for two months now. I think I'm getting in shape." He dug a pack of smokes from a front pocket and lit one. Well, at least all of his bad habits weren't gone yet.

He poked a paw at my wood piles. "You been busy. Wasn't sure what I'd find when I got here. But you're doing okay from the looks of it, Bob."

I too admired my work. "I was worried I was low," I replied, taking a sip of ice-cold water from my Packers thermal mug. "Once I started digging though…" I nodded at the cut wood.

"You got a month's worth there," he offered. "Maybe a month and a half. But you're through the worst of it now. You'll make it."

Dizzy's affirmation of my best guess caused a feeling of pride to swell within my soul. I could feel my chest rise and stick out slightly; pride does that to a man. But I knew pride could be my downfall as well. If I became too complacent with my surroundings and myself, this place could, and most likely would, eat me up in a heartbeat.

"I'm planning a hunting trip next week," Dizzy added, taking a seat on my front bench. "Thought you might want to come out with me for a few days." He peeked up at me through his long hair. "You game?"

The thought of going out into the wild, particularly this

wilderness, for a hunting trip would have caused me to practically wet myself with fear a few months back. This area was too large, too remote, too dangerous for a novice like me. But surviving nearly four months on my own gave me a "can do" sense of accomplishment.

"Yeah," I answered, sounding more sure than I felt. This was Dizzy after all. And trouble could still easily find us. "Couple days, hunt from your place?"

"Yep," he answered, scooping a mitt full of snow from the ground and licking at it. "You head on back in a couple days. We'll get all set up and then hunt from sunrise to sunset; back to my place in the dark. I figure we get a couple deer, that'll put us in a good spot. We can clean 'em, hang 'em, and won't have to worry about them spoiling right away."

"But they'll freeze rock hard," I pointed out, finding a hole in Dizzy's plan.

He grinned, drawing up another hand full of snow. "I got a smoker," he answered, proudly. "We'll smoke them and then that meat will be good for six months. I done it before. Even got some sweet apple wood to burn. It'll take a couple more days, but it'll be good in the end."

So the plan was set. Dizzy would wait for me to arrive; we'd take a couple deer, smoke them, and have another source of protein to last almost to summer.

"I'll see you in two days," he announced as he trudged off on his snowshoes. "If you ain't there, I'll come looking for that skinny sorry ass of yours, so don't make me trudge all the way back here."

"I'll be there!" I shouted after him. "Just be ready, because I'll be there."

Day 123 WOP

Famous last words: This ship is unsinkable (The Titanic). It's just a few Indians (George Custer). Just be ready, because I'll be there (Bob Reiniger).

Gathering the last of the necessary items for my hunting excursion with Dizzy, I paused and stared blankly at my pile. Something was missing.

My coat laid on the couch, stuffed with some essentials. One extra pair of gloves, an extra hat, my woolen scarf that Lettie had so graciously offered me last fall. Next to my coat was my travel pack, also a gift from Lettie. In there were a number of plastic bags of dried fruits and vegetables from Lettie, some jerky given to me by Dizzy, and a plastic jug three-quarters full of brandy. The liquid was a gift from Frank on my last fall visit to his area south of here.

It came to me again that I owed my neighbors a lot. To be honest, I would have been dead by now if not for their generosity. How I would ever repay them had been a quiet argument all winter, if only in my mind.

I snapped my fingers; I had forgotten extra ammo. My

Glock held 15 shells in its magazine. Though my shooting had improved as time inched forward (thanks to three boxes shot up over a five-day period where I was bored during some decent late fall weather) I still needed an extra box, just in case.

Digging the ammo out from its storage spot in the closet, a loud conversation outside caught my attention. I stood and peeked through the bedroom blinds but couldn't see anyone near. Moving to the living room (let's be honest, it was the only other room in the place but I still called it my living room), I waited for someone to appear as the shouting grew louder.

On the road, some 20 yards out, a large man marched, pushing a smaller person along. I'd seen this scene before, and it always went the same. A father, desperate for a better life than just surviving in the woods, urged his child along towards a chance of something more.

This child, like most, argued. And why wouldn't they? Four months ago, they fell asleep in a world that offered them everything. At all times they were connected to social media, whether through laptops, iPads or cell phones. Life was good. Comfortable. Easy.

Then came a sharp right turn. Gone were their friends,

their connectivity, their life (or so they believed).

Parents needed to employ strong measures to keep their children safe. And if that meant dragging them from one small community (such as Covington) where order had disintegrated, to another safe place (like I believed Amasa to be), then so be it.

And so the struggle ensued. More than once I'd met these kinds, strolling down the middle of a formerly busy highway. The parent implored reason; teens despise reason. They see it as a trick. But like the scene before me, the parent always won out.

The conversation became clear to me. And it was as nasty as the ones before.

"Move your scrawny ass," a deep voice shouted. "We gotta make Amasa before nightfall. It ain't safe on these roads after dark."

"I'm not going!" a young voice screeched. "Leave me be!"

Maybe Mom had died; perhaps she'd taken her own life in a world full of mostly despair. And there were likely friends involved. Nearby perhaps, even if that meant a mile or two away. I turned and glanced at the scene, pulling my jacket on. This was their fight, no place for me in it.

I watched as the large man in a brown leather duster

pushed the child along. He towered over her by a good head and a half. There was no way she would win this battle. Even if only out of spite, the child would march along silently in the end.

More shoving ensued. A backhand from the monster knocked the girl to the ground. I became concerned, but it wasn't my fight.

Taking his glove off, I watched as he pulled her up from the road by her stocking cap covered hair. That's when my heart skipped a beat. When the stocking cap came off, I noticed something familiar.

Purple hair.

Day 123 - continued - WOP

Out the door as fast as my legs would allow, I sprinted for the road. Fishing in my right jacket pocket, I dug out the Glock, letting it hang by my side as I approached the kicking and screaming.

Getting within 10 feet before being noticed, I halted and raised the gun.

"Leave her alone," I demanded in a sharp tone.

That got the man's attention. His eyes shifted away from Violet to me. "This is none of your business, pal," he growled. "Piss off."

I raised the gun at him, slapping the gun with my free hand at the last moment. That definitely got his attention. He backed away several steps to the far side of the road, studying the pistol and me through tight eyes.

"This is between me and my daughter, friend," he said, raising both hands slightly, palms opened towards me. "So why don't you just go about your day and leave us alone."

It was only then I noticed the thin twine strung between his waist and Violet's wrists. Though she was trying to make her escape, the short tether wouldn't allow her much distance.

"First, that's not your daughter," I said, taking a step towards the quivering girl. "And I don't know what gives you the right to bind her like that, but I want you to cut that twine right now."

He shrugged, his eyes going between the two, the girl and my gun. I watched him draw a small, thin knife from his side and cut her loose.

Taking her by the arm, I guided her to the far side of the road. "What's going on, Violet?" I asked, helping her pull her wrists free of the old rope.

Shucking her bonds onto the road, she shoved a hand at the man. "I was out gathering wood and this creep comes along and grabs me." The disgust in her voice should have made the man blanch, but instead he grinned.

"You know what a nice young person will bring you at the fish camps they're setting up for next spring?" he answered, acting as if he'd done nothing wrong.

"I have no idea what you're talking about," I replied, shoving Violet behind me on the edge of the road. "And I don't care. She's going back to her parents."

I turned and faced her. "Where's your dad?"

Her eyes were still focused on the ruffian. "He's been sick the last week or so," she replied, shaking her head as she did.

"We're getting low on wood so Mom sent me out to scrounge for dry stuff, for the cook stove, you know. I must have wandered further away from the place than I thought."

I squeezed her arm gently. "Well, you're going back now."

When I turned to face the other again, I noticed it at his side. Larger than mine, yet just as jet black. I watched him cock the hammer.

"She's coming with me," he stated in a low, even tone. "I need her to settle a debt down the road. She'll be fine. All she's gonna do is take a wagon ride to Marquette in a couple weeks and then start cleaning fish."

He turned his head sideways at us. "I ain't gonna hurt her. But I need her. You understand."

Yeah, I understood. He was selling her to the highest bidder. And just as Frank had prognosticated last fall, there'd be all sorts of free labor available by spring. For whatever jobs ruthless people wanted done. Anarchy at its finest…and worst.

"She's going home," I replied, watching his gun. Though it hung at his side, I knew that could change in a heartbeat.

"I'm taking her, even if that means killing you, friend." This guy had no intention of backing down, though I was praying hard he might.

"I don't want to kill you," I replied, trying to reason with a desperate man.

He glared at me and me alone now. "If you don't give her to me, I *will* kill you."

With an eye on his gun, I guided Violet a little further away from the pending battle. "Stay over here," I said, loud enough for the stranger to hear. "I don't want you getting caught in the middle of this."

He grinned again, licking at his long dirty mustache. "You may as well have her stand over here," he said, laughing as he spoke. "That way when I kill you I can tie her up again. Make it easier on the both of us."

My breath came in stuttered spurts. My heart pounded so loudly, I could hear each beat push against my eardrums. Yet I willed myself to stay cool on the outside, refusing to show any fear.

"Leave," I said forcefully. "Head down that road and never come back." I took several small steps further away from Violet. He measured my movements with tiny slits of eyes, waiting for the moment.

"Just so you know," he stated from maybe 20 feet away, "I don't get no joy out of killing another. Why don't you just turn around and run off? Save us both a lot of misery."

So that was the way he wanted it. Either I ran off like a

coward, or he'd gun me down where I stood. Not much of a choice, I figured. Maybe back six months ago, I would have already been a half-mile down the road, running until my legs and lungs gave out.

But the image of her family stayed glued at the front of my mind. They deserved better from me. And even if I died, at least I tried. I'd want someone to do the same for my family. I would do the same for Violet's.

"Doesn't have to be this way," he growled, stepping back into the ditch on the far side of the road. I mirrored his movements.

Finally, I nodded. "Yeah, it does."

Day 123 - continued - WOP

My father sat me down one day and gave a lesson in life. To this day, I think of it all the time.

"In any negotiation, son, the person that mentions price loses." He ended it with a hearty nod and by patting my hands. "First guy who flinches is usually the loser. You have to learn to be patient, Robert."

A few years later, I went to buy my first car. It was a used junker and the man was asking way too much for something in that rough of shape. Still I wanted it; I wanted it bad.

"So, what'll you give me for it?" the seller asked, trying to sound like he wouldn't take a penny less than what he posted it for.

I almost answered right away, almost. One thousand ran through my mind, but that was a lowball, and I knew it. Then I decided to offer $1,500, something more reasonable. But as I opened my mouth, Dad's advice shot through my mind.

"What do you really want for it?" I asked, trying to sound as uninterested as possible.

Within five minutes he signed the title over to me and I handed him a stack of hundred dollar bills, eight of them.

Dad wasn't always right, but he was that time.

Watching the man's gun instead of his eyes, I felt my breathing slow. I didn't want to kill him. I'd killed once already and that was enough for a lifetime. But I wasn't backing down. And I knew he'd either give in and leave or raise his weapon. I let Dad's words echo in my thoughts…*Be patient, Robert.*

His gun came up quick, almost catching me off-guard. He fired a wild shot that didn't cause me pain, so I assumed he missed.

I fired quickly, not even aiming the gun. Simply point and pull. I saw snow kick up in the ditch two feet to his right, about knee high.

He scurried for one ditch, firing three times as he did. I did the same on my side of the road, only getting off one shot in response.

Six shots had been fired at close range, less than 10 yards between us. Yet the only thing taking hits was the woods beyond each of us. Off to my right, I watched Violet make a mad dash into the woods, settling behind a windfall maybe 20 yards away.

The man shot twice more and I sensed he was zeroing in on me. I rose to fire again but he was ready. His shot struck me in the left side, knocking me on my back into the ditch.

A flurry of activity took up the next few seconds. Though I wasn't sure where he'd hit me, I knew it was bad. Beside me, I noticed the snow peppered with red splotches of my blood. Nearer to my body was a pool of it, melting the snow as I bled out.

I heard him approach, his gun extended at me. From the center of the road, he fired again. Snow and dirt blew up beside my face, maybe three inches away. Close enough to make me scream.

Feeling my own pistol still clutched in my right hand, I jerked it up as he stepped even closer. Squeezing three shots off in rapid succession, I was greeted by another shot from his gun. This one missed my right hip by a foot. When I went to pull the trigger again, I saw him collapse to the ground. I had no idea which shot hit him, but one had knocked him down.

I went to push off with my left hand when the pain blinded me. Staring down I saw the crimson snow, no longer white anywhere near my wound. I needed to be sure this was over, but my situation was desperate, I was in trouble.

A hand jerked my gun away. When I looked back, I saw Violet, gun in hand, rushing towards the moaning man. She pointed the weapon at him.

"I said I wasn't going anywhere with you!" *Bang!* "I told you to leave me alone!" *Bang!* "You're nothing but a stupid creep!" *Bang!*

After drawing a deep breath, I silently watched Violet spit on the dead body. I didn't know for sure at that point if he was dead, but she had shot him three more times, at point blank range. So I just assumed…

"Wow, that's a lot of blood," she said, kneeling next to me. "Where were you hit?" Her eyes studied my wound, my eyes stayed glued to her.

"In the side somewhere," I moaned, reaching for the gun with my free hand. Thankfully, she gave it up without a struggle. "Is he…?" No need to ask the obvious, not all the way at least.

She glanced back at the road. "Yeah, I shot him in the middle of the chest," she admitted, pulling my jacket up as she did. "Three times." Violet sighed loudly. "Mom says I have anger issues." I felt her warm hand on my side. "I suppose she could be right."

Yeah, she did. But we had other issues that needed our immediate attention.

"Where'd he hit me?" I asked. Watching her face go through a range of contortions, I could only assume I was soon to be a dead man.

"Well, there's a lot of blood, but I don't see any hole in your side." Gently, she tugged at my glove and that sent a shock wave through my body.

"Crap," she shouted. "You're shot in the hand. Quick bury it in the snow, it's bleeding everywhere."

I would have thought the instant contact with the cold snow would have eased my immediate pain. Instead, another bolt of hideous pain worked its way up my arm to my head.

"We gotta get you back inside so we can stop the bleeding," she said, pulling at me to help me sit up. "Then I gotta go get mom. She's a nurse and she has stuff. She'll be able to help you."

On my feet, I almost threw up. Looking down, a string of gooey blood hung from my glove. Where I had been lying, a lot more blood covered the snow.

I glanced at Violet as she led me home. "How can you stay so calm in all of this?" I asked, trying to keep my swimming vision from overtaking me.

"I've seen worse," she answered. I wasn't sure how that was possible, but my mind wouldn't focus on anything but the pain, and the swirling woods my world had become.

"Come on," she said, encouraging me along. "Just a few

more steps…"

That's the last I remember from that day.

Day 129 WOP

I came into consciousness in fits over the next few days. And never more than a few minutes at a time.

I remember the door slamming as Violet ran to get help. Mostly I remember that because I was sure I was going to die. I recalled her and Marge hovering over me. Great bolts of pain rendered me unconscious again when they removed my glove.

I recalled the stink of burning flesh and screams. I think they were my screams…something they had done to my hand. Water was poured down my throat as I choked on some kind of pills either Marge or Violet coaxed me to swallow.

Then I remember nothing. Not even dreams.

I awoke days later to the strangest sound I'd ever heard. It sounded like rain, which was impossible, unless I'd slept the rest of winter away. Forcing my eyes open, pain found its way back inside my head.

I actually couldn't decide which hurt worse: my wounded hand or the stabbing at my eyes. I laid my head back down and drifted off. Until I heard singing. At that point I knew I was either delusional or dead.

A thin figure in a pink fuzzy bathrobe stood before me. On its feet were matching fuzzy bunny slippers, its head wrapped in a clean white towel.

"Are you hungry?" a feminine voiced asked. I felt her hand on my forehead. "I think your temperature is almost back to normal."

She leaned closer, her nose almost touching mine. Her breath smelled like wintergreen.

"We need to get you up and moving," she added softly. "And you smell pretty ripe. You could stand to clean up."

Even then, I had no idea who my angel was. Her touch was kind and gentle, her voice the same. I saw the towel whip around her head as she whistled back into the kitchen. Several tussles through her hair and as the towel lowered, I saw the hair.

"What are you doing here, Violet?" I asked, my voice croaking from non-use.

She picked up something from the counter and sipped at it. I could see steam as it drifted away. "Mom left me here to watch after you," she answered, raking her boncy fingers through her still wet hair. "We knew you weren't going to die, just needed watching. So she told me to stay, since you rescued me and all."

Rubbing my eyes with my right hand, I noticed the bandage on my left. While I expected it to be blood-soaked and dripping, I was surprised it was as white as the new snow outside the cabin.

"You lost a finger," she stated, standing over me again. She pointed at her own left hand, slightly more delicate than my own. "Your pinky, right at the base. I'm sorry."

She sounded sincere, almost like she really cared.

"How many days…?" I asked, hoping I didn't need to finish the sentence.

She smiled at me, taking a bite of what looked to be some type of homemade cookie.

"Six," she answered plainly. "Do you remember anything?"

Shaking my head, I leaned back on the soft pillow that someone must have brought for me to use.

"The gunfight, the red snow, the smell of burning flesh. Maybe someone shoving things down my throat."

She rose and stared at me. "Those were pills so you didn't get an infection. Mom took them from the nursing home she worked at before we left Covington. The smell was from when she cauterized your wound…so you wouldn't bleed to death."

Violet had a way of making things sound so matter of fact.

Probably her youth and her level of boredom watching a man sleep for six days.

"There was a lot of blood in the snow," she continued. "I almost threw up when I first saw it, then my first aid training kicked in."

She knelt beside me, feeling my forehead again. "And this is really important, okay?" I nodded. "You can't tell anyone about me shooting that guy. Mom will have a major episode if she finds out I pulled the trigger, too. You gotta promise."

I shrugged. She'd probably saved my life; a little bending of the truth seemed like a fair trade.

"How many times was he hit?" I asked, watching the pink robe wander back towards the sink. "You shot him three times; how many times did I hit him?"

Holding up a single finger, Violet almost looked disappointed for me…or with me. "But you hit him in the throat. So that was a good shot."

Yeah, great shot. I was aiming dead center at his chest when I pulled the trigger.

"Where's your mom?"

Leaning over the fire, she played with her hair a little more. "Taking care of Dad. He has a bug of some sort."

"That's why you were in the woods, that's right." Some of

this was coming back to me.

"Bury your head," Violet requested. "I need to get dressed and I don't want you perving on me."

"How is it possible…it looks like you took a shower?" Wet hair, humidity in the air, and she appeared clean.

Tearing back the shower curtain on the tiny stall in the corner, she pointed up. "Mom and I rigged up a bucket with holes. We did the same at our pit. Warm up some water on the stove, pour it into the bucket and you have three gallons of clean water. You just need to be quick."

I rolled over, burying my head in the soft feather pillow. "You should use the bedroom," I said. "That would give you more privacy."

"Yeah," she sputtered. "Blood stained mattress, the smell of death. I'll take my chances out here."

All fall, I'd put off dragging that mattress outside. Since I slept on the couch every night, it didn't matter, until now.

"And who is that creepy man who keeps showing up?" she asked, the sound of jeans being pulled on filling the air.

"That would most likely be Dizzy." Crap, that's what I was forgetting. I was supposed to be going hunting with him.

"Well, he's coming back tomorrow to check on you. I'm going to run and go get Mom to check up on your wound, make sure it's healing okay." I turned over and she stood by the door, pulling on the same coat I had first seen going down the highway. More memories flooded back.

"How come you're staying with me?" I asked. She owed me nothing that I could think of. What I'd done for her, anyone would have.

Drawing a deep breath, she floated me a mischievous grin. "I get time away from the family this way. It's been rough being cooped up in a small place like we're at. Here I can read, or draw, or do whatever I want. There, Mom always has some boring chore lined up for me."

She reached for the knob, but stopped mid-turn. "Plus, what you did for me…that was pretty cool. You're okay. I'll be back in two hours. Try to eat something by then, okay?"

I watched her disappear around the corner of the yard and down the road. While I'd prefer slightly older company, Violet's mostly mature attitude was fine for the time being.

I stared at the shower. Maybe that would make me feel better.

Day 172 WOP

Marge decided it was mid-February, though I had thought that was the month before. Nearly half of a year was gone and I found myself in a similar spot. No Where, the place where I'd almost died a few months back.

While I was unconscious, Violet found my calendar and marked the time for me. Somewhere in the middle of her one-month stay, she confessed to maybe missing a day or two. Truth be told, I knew I had missed a few myself.

It didn't really matter anymore, time. Or how we formerly perceived time. Days came and went. Months did the same. Once upon a time, at the start of winter, I spent most of my waking hours thinking about home. Now, weeks passed before I could recall any of Shelly's features.

My wife was small and slight, that much I remembered. Just how small and slight, that was not as clear. My only younger female reference for the past half of a year was Violet, and she was 13. And not a big 13. No, she too was small and slight.

Violet claimed to be 5-2. Okay, that made Shelly 5-5 I thought. But was she only three inches taller than the waif that chased after me every time I bumped the stump on the end of my left hand, trying to stop the bleeding? I couldn't recall. Shelly had blonde hair, sort of. Maybe more sandy blonde, the type of color somewhere between golden blonde and all-out brown.

Shelly's teeth were straight. Braces had been slapped on at an early age and she still wore a retainer to bed the last night I remembered from home. She had a lotion that she covered herself in before bed that smelled like honeysuckle. I could almost smell it, sitting on the couch, watching the snow fall again.

I remembered waking up to the fresh fragrance found in my wife's hair. I never knew what shampoo she used; we had separate bathrooms and showers. When we did shower together, I was too busy with other things to do something as mundane as seek out her cleanser.

The bottle left in my crude shower in the cabin had the same fragrance. It drove me insane each time I caught a whiff of it. I wept alone at night, wondering if I would be home again, not here home but truly home.

My injury had a dreaded repercussion on my body — I'd lost a lot of weight. And just from a gunshot to the hand. I wondered how much more I would have wasted away if I had been shot in the thorax.

Once spring came, I had hoped to be on the road, Chicago bound. But the loss of significant weight made that seem like a dream. I'd first have to gain back the weight and strength required for a 400-mile walk. I had resized my belt twice already during this time. The slack on my waist signaled another round was due.

"You're gonna have to put on twenty pounds at least," Dizzy warned on one of his afternoon visits. "If you plan on making that trip, that is."

Sitting next to him on the couch, I heard the concern his tone may or may not have intended to leak.

"I need to try," I countered, depression filling my soul.

"I get it. I do. But," he paused, seeming to search for the right phrase, "you might not make it, you know. People are claiming the roads will be full of vultures this spring. Desperate people, desperate times."

"I need Shelly," I stated. But he'd heard this all before, many times. "I need my wife."

"You could have Marge, now that Warren's gone," he replied, trying to give me options.

Warren's bug turned out to be a serious infection caused by a wood saw he scraped across his leg. By the time Marge discovered the true source of the fever, two weeks had passed. A week later, Dizzy dug his shallow grave in the still frozen snowscape.

"They all moved in with Lettie, you know," he added. "She's been pretty depressed ever since. You two could hit it off."

"I'm not interested in a romance with Marge, Dizzy. She's almost twice my age."

"What about Violet? She seems pretty sweet on you."

My mouth dropped open as I glared at my friend. "I'm not interested in a child either. I want Shelly."

He shifted on the couch, away from me, sensing my irritation with his ideas. "Lettie says there's trouble all over. Covington's rotten, Amasa is bad. She even heard word that Green Bay has been overrun by some kind of flu. People dying in droves down there. Everywhere I guess."

And that left me here, smack dab in the middle of Shit's Creek. Too weak to run, too strong to die.

"There's got to be more than just surviving, Dizzy. There has to be."

He rose and strolled to the window. "Another man came through last week. Had a dozen followers or so. You see them on the road?"

I nodded once. I had seen their group, all dressed in dark clothes, looking like their last bath came days before this all happened. But I didn't give a damn about whatever kind of crap they might be spreading.

"Word is that what that fellow told Frank late last summer was God's honest truth," Dizzy continued, wiping away some dust from the sill with a finger. "The whole country is down, no power anywhere. Some people seen some older running vehicles on the road, here and there. I sure ain't seen any myself. No phones neither. Says its real bad everywhere. God's wrath or something like that. Might even be worldwide."

"Bull shit," I answered, refusing to even peek in his direction.

"Some say the nuclear plants melted down after the power went out. Half the country is covered in radiation." I heard him approach my spot. "Thought about that? There's plants like that all around Lake Michigan. It could be real deadly south of here. This may be the safest place in the country right now."

I glared at him and his rumors sold as logic. None of this was new to me. I wrote it off as Dizzy not wanting to lose a friend and nothing more.

"It can't be like that. It just can't be."

He shrugged away my tense words. "Why not?"

"Because I need hope, Dizzy. I need the hope that someday I'll get out of this place."

Shaking his head at me, he made his way to the door.

"Remember what they say about hope, Bob. You can crap in one hand and hope in the other. But you know damn well which one is gonna fill up first." I heard the door creak open. "I'll see you tomorrow. Hang in there."

Damn him, damn his logic. And damn this world if that's how bad it's become.

Day 245 WOP

Spring arrived with a thunderstorm just before dawn. The rolling thunder mixed in with the last of my dreams, and damn they were good dreams.

I was at a backyard cookout at my place. Everyone was there. Shelly and my friends, both of our parents, my brother Bud, her kid sister Molly (who hated Bud with a passion, not that he ever figured that out), and even some of the neighbors we had an occasional beer with.

There were brats and burgers on the grill. God they smelled good. The beer boiling the brats was full of onions and a stick of butter. The pungent hops, mixing with the sweet onions and butter. Then the hearty medium-rare well-seared burgers. With buns the size of dinner plates, toasted and buttered.

I manned the grill, flipping burgers, stirring the brats occasionally, and sharing jokes with Dad and Bud. It was as if I were really there.

Shelly had set a beautiful table with bright red plates and a billowing white tablecloth. The setting was serene. The sun was setting, birds were chirping, and in the corner of the backyard, several rabbits ate in our garden. Shelly laughed, seeing them chomp at her lettuce. Normally she would have chased them away with a broom. But for some reason, she found them entertaining and quaint.

When it came time to eat, I made an extra plate up and snuck inside. In the corner of the living room sat Frank, in his chair from home. I spread a napkin on his lap and laid the plate on top of it.

"I'm happy you're here, Frank," I said, watching him stir the gooey brown beans with his cragged finger.

He looked up at me, his face tight with either anger or concern — I couldn't decide which it was.

"There's a storm coming," he replied, his voice booming. "You need to be ready, and you're not."

In the distance, I heard the thunder. When I turned to the window, lightning streaked across the now dark sky, blackened by storm clouds. The wind blew strong, tossing the plates and cups from the elegant table.

When I turned back to my friend, he and his chair were gone. In their place, the carpet smoldered. Stomping my foot on the charred carpet, flames erupted below me. I went to scream, but thunder muffled my cries.

Bolting up on the couch, I shook the dream from my head. Outside, rain ran from the roof like someone had turned on a giant hose. Though I knew it was morning, well after sunrise, the storm clouds made it look like evening. Another round of lightning followed by thunder brought me to full consciousness.

It was time to go visit Frank.

If I were honest about things, Frank was the closest thing I had to a father up here. Though he was ornery and argumentative with most, he always treated me decently. When he spoke, I could tell he was the kind of a man who'd lived by the golden rule: treat others as you wished to be treated. Frank was a real no bullshit kind of guy. I liked that about him.

If Frank was my wilderness father figure, that made Lettie my mother. Even though she'd never wed, never bore a child, had very few kin (as she called them), she was still a loving, caring human being. Her iffy past life meant nothing any longer. That was then, it was what she had to do to live, and it was over.

It seemed almost comical to me that Frank and Lettie knew one another from the old days; Frank a salty sailor, Lettie the local favorite at the strip club. Even with their sullied pasts, they remained lifelong friends. That told me something about these people, about their characters, about their souls.

Dizzy was the cousin that no one wanted to admit being related to. His exterior was hard to get past. Through and through, he was a woodsman. He acted like one, lived like one, even smelled like one. He was unique, no way around that. But he was a loyal friend.

Many times, mostly at night as I planned my escape, I wondered what life would be like without this trio. Though they had no reason to, they had shown me kindness, support and generosity in a time when others turned away strangers. And that's what I had been to them.

Waiting for the rain to end, I packed a bag to take to Frank. I had a treat for him, besides the six jars of venison that probably needed to be eaten. Declaring Marge's depression over, Lettie turned her loose in the kitchen and cookies began to appear on my doorstep. Crumbly tan sugar cookies. I figured Frank would enjoy a dozen or so.

Day 247 WOP

Two days of off-again, on-again rain kept me inside my cabin. I was going to Frank's, but I wasn't trudging through downpours that would leave me soaked for days.

The rain had washed away the last of winter's white, I noticed. Here and there in the woods I saw a few remnants of snow, but the road was clear. Walking was a whole lot easier without putting on the small pink boots, though I did detect a hole starting at the front of my sneakers.

Dizzy and I were going to have to go "shopping" soon. That's what Dizzy called his planned raids on nearby vacant cottages. Pillaging was probably a better description. But it wasn't like someone would be showing up anytime soon to visit their vacation hideaway. So I adopted Dizzy's logic; what these folks would never know was fine. No one got hurt in the deal.

The trees along the road with their skeleton arms moved softly in the breeze. It would be another month before leaves appeared, according to Dizzy. As best as anyone could tell, it was somewhere around April 15th. A smile lit my face as the sunshine warmed my soul. Tax day, but not this year. Perhaps never again.

Walking down the middle of the highway, a thought came to me. Frank knew nothing of my injured hand. I wondered what his expression would be when I showed him the missing digit. Would he laugh, would he cuss out rotten people, or would he simply take a hit of brandy and tell me, 'That's the way it goes sometimes?'

My stamina was low, so the trip took longer than normal. I heard my stomach grumble as I rounded the last bend before my destination. Maybe one of these jars of venison would have to be eaten right away, along with several cookies. Yeah, sugar cookies and tepid brandy. That sounded okay.

I stopped short when Frank's place came into view. Studying the scene carefully, I noticed the front screen porch door open, shifting back and forth with the wind. I patted my pocket and found the Glock. Pulling it out, I approached with caution. Gone were the hunger pains, replaced by a tight feeling in my gut.

The house felt cold, as if no fire had burned in the past week, maybe longer. Aside from the screen door being opened, the main door sat ajar as well. Something wasn't right here.

I called Frank's name several times, shouting the last time.

No response.

The place looked picked over. Every cupboard door was open. His pantry had been raided. Only a single half-full jar of peanut butter was left, sitting alone on the middle shelf. Whoever grabbed Frank's food didn't want peanut butter.

Creeping down the back hall, I checked one bedroom, empty, then the bathroom, which was also vacant. That just left the final door at the end of the hall. The room I believed to be Frank's.

For some stupid reason, I knocked on the white painted door and called his name again. I guess it was just a courtesy, my proper upbringing coming through even when my skin crawled with fear.

Opening the door, the smell hit me first, causing me to pull my gloved bad hand to my face, covering my nose. It was easy to find the source of the smell. The terrible smell of death. Frank splayed in his bed, covered to his chest with a white comforter. His glasses laid on the bedside nightstand, his arms by his sides.

To another, it might have appeared he was sleeping. But I knew better; Frank was dead.

Withdrawing to the living room, I choked back emotions that begged for release. Foul play hadn't happened here. Sure, maybe some road trash came to the door, knocked and when no reply was offered, they came inside. They took what little Frank had to offer.

Maybe they even looked in the closed room. But if the sight of a dead man didn't deter them, the rotting corpse most certainly would have.

I went to his hiding spot where he kept a bottle at all times. Fishing around the corner of the cupboard, deep inside the dark recesses that held white china plates with matching cups, I found his stash. Pulling the half-full bottle out, I noticed an envelope taped to its round, clear edges.

The scratchy, jagged handwriting read one word: *Bob*.

Bob,

Hopefully, it's you who found me. The last thing I need is for a bunch of strangers digging through my house. Even worse than that if my numbskull nephew finds me, hell, he'll try and bury me. That ain't what I want.

I built this place back in the late 60s with my wife, Isabel. She and I were married 47 years before she died a decade and a half ago. Missed her every day since. But the point is, this place is mine. Not no one else.

When I worked on the big ships out on Superior, which I did for a great many years, I slipped one day and broke two vertebrae in my back. Besides surgery, they gave me Valium for the pain. God, it's a wonderful drug. I've been hooked ever since I took my first taste. It was the one thing that eased the pain.

A few mornings ago, I began to search my stash for more pills. Thought I had another bottle or two hidden somewhere. Turns out I was wrong. I was working on the last bunch I'd ever have. That scared me straight.

If things went as planned, I took somewhere between 15 and 20 painkillers all at once. If that didn't kill me, I'm too ornery to die. But I'm betting it did.

Don't shed a single tear for me, 'cuz I wouldn't for you. I'm old, I'm tired, I miss my wife and I'm ready to go. And ain't gonna live on some hope that you or that dipshit Dizzy will show up and go steal me more pills. No sir. I'm going out my way.

You know where I keep the key to my root cellar. Go get it and clean the place out. Take that bow my nephew left behind, too. Should be good for killing deer. And I've tucked my 45 under my pillow, just in case someone breaks in while I'm still with it. Man never knows anymore.

Everything you want that I have left is yours. I got a cart out back you can load the stuff into and haul it back to your place. Probably gonna take you half a dozen trips, maybe two days. But when you got all you want, you need to repay my kindness with one last act.

Take that stack of old newspapers I keep out on the front porch and pile them around the living room. There's about a quarter of a gallon of gas out back in the shed. Coat the papers well but watch out for the fumes. You should probably toss a burning rag in through the front window. No need in two of us going up in flames.

Do it, damn it. Don't think about it, just do it. It's what I want.

What I don't want is a bunch of strangers moving into the place that Isabel and I called home for so many years. That would be the worst way to honor my death. And I really don't want a bunch of vultures picking my bones clean because a bunch of idiots tossed me out back in the swamp.

Before you think of doing anything stupid, let an old man give you some advice. That dipshit nephew of mine always warned me about nuclear hazards. If what we think has happened has happened, it's gonna be bad most places. Avoid Green Bay, avoid the Twin Cities, avoid Milwaukee and Chicago both. Stay in the UP, Bob. It may be the last decent place left on earth now.

Live because you're pissed off at God, or humanity or whatever gets your blood pumping. But live, and live a good long life, like I have — just minus the drugs. Those things will mess with your mind.

Tell Lettie she was the best stripper I ever met. Though she already knows that, I think it will make her smile knowing I was thinking of her at the end. Tell Dizzy to lose some weight and quit smoking. I'm surprised he's outlived me already. And if my nephew ever comes around looking for me, tell him to go to hell. He always treated me like a free lunch.

Goodbye.

Your friend,
Franklin Peter Morgan

Day 252 WOP

Using Frank's well-constructed cart, it took three days to haul away the usable items from his root cellar. That place, by the way, was a treasure trove full of goodies.

He had managed to accumulate full crates of canned food. Most were vegetables; he always claimed that they were the key to his long, healthy life. But there was more.

It became apparent that Frank was a lover of pork and beans. One certain variety of the stuff. Almost one full crate held more than 30 cans of the still edible legumes. Those were going to be tasty, and last quite a while.

In a corner, I found two full boxes of 45 caliber handgun shells. Each box contained 50 separate containers holding 20 shells apiece. That meant I now had a gun with 2,000 rounds of ammo. Thank you, Frank. Thank you very, very much.

Jars of venison and bear lined one wall, along with a large quantity of canned meat. Those shelves alone cost me a day of travel. Articles of old clothing, several pairs of boots, boxes and boxes of stick matches, and other items necessary for my survival made the trips. Did I say my survival? I meant our survival.

On the last trip, I piled the cart full of any other remnants of Frank's days I thought might be useful. The final item I loaded was a Bear compound bow, along with four dozen arrows, left behind by Frank's nephew.

All items were hauled almost 10 miles to Lettie's place. There we could take our time and sort through our bounty. She had extra storage; I had a tiny place with an unusable bedroom that still contained a blood-soaked mattress. Eventually, I'd need to fix that problem, but not until I was finished with Frank's wishes.

"Are you sure about this?" Dizzy asked as we filled Frank's home with crumpled newspapers. "I mean it seems kind of odd, if you ask me."

I kept at my task, stuffing some wads under the couch. "It's what he wanted. His last wish."

A chair cracked as Dizzy took a seat. "I knew Frank a long time. He was always a half-bubble off plumb if you ask me."

That caused me to grin. The feeling was mutual, I knew.

"Okay, you got the gas?" I asked, knowing everything was ready.

"You want to go look at him one last time?" Dizzy asked, rising from his spot.

No, I didn't. And it wasn't because dead people bothered

me. I'd seen plenty in my life. Two grandmas, three grandpas (I guess one was actually a step-grandpa), numerous great-aunts and uncles. Dead people were just that — dead, lifeless. Plus, I'd already said my goodbyes to Frank.

"Can't stand the smell, Dizzy. He's been dead a while, so it isn't pretty." I peeked back at him. "But if you want to, be my guest."

The man lost all color in his face. "God no. I hate dead people I know. Gives me the willies. Let's just get this done."

A half hour later, we stood in the middle of the deserted highway, watching the flames lick through the shattered windows. Inside, what was left of Frank was being released. Just as he wanted.

Dizzy and I passed a bottle back and forth, taking hits, wiping away whatever tears Frank didn't want.

"I guess the old coot got his wish," Dizzy said, passing me the brandy again. "He was always a stubborn prick."

I laughed, then coughed as liquor burned my throat. "He claimed you were a dipshit." I peeked back as Dizzy chased away a final tear. A grin covered his face.

"Yeah, I liked him too," he admitted, putting his arm around my shoulder, steering me away.

Little was said as we walked home. Besides our shoes crunching gravel on the side of the road, then only sound we made was the occasional slosh from the brandy bottle as we raised it in Frank's memory.

Day 295 WOP

Carrying a mesh bag, I followed my leader on this hunt. Though she said she was capable of doing it alone, I needed to talk to her.

"How do you know which ones are edible?" I asked, watching her pick through several bunches of wild mushrooms.

Plucking several from the dirt, she placed them in the bag. "Just do," Marge answered, shrugging away the question. "My mother and father taught me and my sister from the time we were little."

"You know all the names?" I decided to keep the conversation flowing now that she was actually speaking. Truth was, she hadn't said a lot to either Lettie or me since Warren's death.

"Just what we called them," she replied, walking ahead of me, never looking back.

I followed like an obedient puppy, waiting for the right time to pop the question. "Can I ask you something?" I continued after a long silence.

"I wish you wouldn't," she replied, stopping but not turning around.

"Nate talks about the bad men, a lot. Is he referring to what happened in Covington?"

Still she didn't turn around.

"What does it matter," she whispered just loud enough for me to hear.

"Was it that bad?"

She turned, staring at me, emotionless. "Yes, it was that bad."

"Maybe he needs to talk about it, that's all I'm saying." I thought about reaching to touch her arm, or rub her shoulder. But the emptiness on her face told me it wouldn't do any good.

"He needs to forget; he's young enough. He can forget." She sounded desperate.

"Are they coming?"

Her eyes flared for just a brief second before going back to her dirty hands.

"Violet says they are," I added with a finished tone. "That's why I ask."

"What else do you know?" It was a question, wrapped in a demand that could easily be followed by shrieking. The little bits and piece I received from her children were haunting.

That's why Marge looked like she did: scared, exhausted, almost dead.

"You know she killed the man who tried to kill me." She nodded, her lips trembling. "And she did it in a rather efficient manner. And it didn't seem to bother her." I let the silence attempt to elicit Marge's reply.

"And?" Either she wasn't much of a conversationalist, or she was hiding something. And a bet of three cans of pork and beans told me it was the later.

"Has she killed before? Maybe after things went to hell in Covington?"

For the first time, I noticed the anger in her eyes. "She was protecting a friend. The man was hurting her. Violet had to do something, even if it was heinous."

"So that's why the bad people are coming, for her." I knew it already; I just wanted confirmation before all hell broke loose.

She nodded and then sat on a nearby stump. "That, and all the drugs I took from the nursing home," Marge admitted. "I knew they were looking for them. They were going to use them for some kind of trade. But I had hidden them. I knew we'd need them after our escape."

"Why haven't they shown up yet, these bad people?"

She looked flustered, her lips twisting from side to side, a tic forming on the right side of her face. "I have no idea. Maybe they're waiting for decent weather. Maybe it took them a while to figure out who murdered their man, who exactly took the drugs."

Something didn't sound right. Even if everything were as Marge tried to sell it, why would anyone look for them here?

She must have read my mind. "We left a note of where we were going with a neighbor," she continued. "I hadn't seen them since everything went bad. And I figured if they showed up, they'd know where to find us."

"Maybe the neighbor didn't rat you out. Ever think of that?"

She sighed and rose from her spot. "Maybe they didn't. But if they threatened to rape their daughters, cut them off from any food or water, how long would you hold out? Friend or not, since my parents haven't found us, I expect the next people to come looking will have revenge on their minds."

I let out a huge *whoosh* of air I didn't realize I'd been holding. "Shit," I muttered as we began our trip back to Lettie's.

Marge stopped and pushed my hair away from my face. "Yes, shit."

Day 306 WOP

Trusting a 13-year-old killer with scissors near my face and neck didn't really bother me. Violet did what she had to do if only to protect her friends. Even if only a little less than a year ago, she would have been locked away for her actions.

My scalp had been itching for the past two weeks. Upon further investigation, Lettie discovered the culprit: lice. Lice, in both my hair and beard. They and most of the hair had to go. Enter Miss Violet and her self-professed talents with hair.

She began with long chops at the back of my neck. Watching nearly a foot of brown hair fall to the ground, it reminded me of watching my grandmother cut my grandfather's hair at home. He was far too cheap to pay $1 (at the time) for a decent haircut, so Grandma always did it.

Of course, she'd never actually killed anyone. Either by three gunshots to the chest or a knife to the throat. Violet was quick to point out that the man she killed on the road was half-dead to begin with. So it wasn't actually all on her.

The man she had protected her friend against was actually killed by the other girl's boyfriend. According to Violet, all she had done was grab the man by the scalp and pull his head back. The boyfriend had plunged the knife into his throat.

"Mom never lets me cut anyone's hair at home," Violet complained, attacking the top of my head. While I assumed she would have a gentle touch, I assumed incorrectly. She pulled the comb through an area that hadn't been groomed in about six months.

"Of course, I usually snuck over to Stacy's anytime anyone needed a trim and didn't have money for the salon." I felt the edge of the scissors nick my head, causing me to jerk. "You need to sit still." She emphasized her point by thwacking the side of my head with her stiff comb.

Her fingers dug through what was left on my head. "Whatever Lettie did to those lice, there ain't none now," she added, coming around the front to size up my beard.

"Kerosene," Lettie called from the other room. "Nothing much in this world that good ol' kerosene can't cure."

"Yeah, and my scalp felt like it was on fire," I countered, recalling her dousing me with the liquid. "I traded itching for burning."

Standing in the doorway, leaning against one side, Lettie grinned. "But the lice are dead, and now you can heal. And it wouldn't hurt you to clean up every once in a while."

The days between showers in the makeshift stall were easier

counted as weeks. Once the water warmed up in the lake, I would take bathing there. But as best we could tell, it was only June 1st. We had a few weeks to go before the water warmed up enough.

And that homemade shower was a pain in the butt. It actually took two sessions to get clean. One to get wet and soaped up, and a second to rinse as much of the soap away as you could. I was sick of standing around naked, waiting for the second batch to warm for use. So showers weren't high on my list of priorities.

Thus, the lice. And patchy, flaking skin. Maybe Lettie had a point.

Short hair and free of lice, I walked home midday. Spending time with others helped keep me sane, I knew that much. But spending too much time with them made me feel a little crazy as well.

Lettie was fine, for the most part. Besides being generous with food and aid, she was overly generous with advice as well. I hated when my mom or dad tried to shove their knowledge down my throat. And an older woman I'd known for nearly a year? That wasn't my idea of fun.

Shelly claimed I was too independent. Maybe she had a

point. But in my defense, I knew what I was doing…most of the time. When in doubt, I asked. Hell, I'd made it this long pretty much on my own.

Then there was Marge. If she wasn't walking around like a zombie, add in depression, she was off somewhere crying. I got it, really I did. She missed her husband, was scared for her family and her own safety, and let Lettie make most of the decisions lately.

One thing Shelly was not was a weeper. And rarely was her mood anything but cheery. Hell, she'd sent me north with an amazing long kiss, rubbed my face, and told me to unwind. The time away would do me good, she claimed. I often wondered now how she felt about her encouraging our separation.

Another thing I had no time for was teenagers. In Violet's defense, that meant girls *and* boys. And this teen was no different. One moment everything would be fine, the next, screaming and tossing silverware around. Sometimes I could speak with her rationally. Then, mere moments later, she spewed vitriol in my direction. She wasn't my kid, so let her mother or new "grandma" (Lettie) deal with her gargantuan mood swings.

The boy was fine in my estimation. He knew his dad was

gone and not coming back. I can't say he was happy about the situation, but he seemed to make the best of it. He was eight and resilient. But he also needed a man around.

That man couldn't be me, at least not all the time. At 25 I wasn't qualified, in my mind, to be a father of a newborn baby. An eight-year-old lad? Full of energy and questions? No. That was more Dizzy's speed.

Day 311 WOP

Another thunderstorm was approaching No Where. This one waited for mid-morning to strike, though I noticed the dark clouds on the horizon long before the first drops of rain kicked up the dust on the road for me to smell.

Being cooped inside my small cabin was actually a blessing. I had a few problems to figure out. And no better time than when the weather doesn't want you out cutting wood, hunting game or working in Lettie's garden.

First was my trip home. The mere mention of this to my small band of friends brought tears, and moans, and gnashing of teeth.

They claimed I needed to stay. They even insisted it was for my safety, but I knew better. Lettie and Marge both wanted a man around, even if he lived three miles away.

"But I have a life back in Chicago," I stated during our latest argument, spreading fertilizer in Lettie's massive garden.

"You'll have no life if you leave," Lettie warned, waving her cigarette at me. "You might make it as far as Green Bay, but the road trash will eat you up if radiation doesn't get you first."

Leaning on a four-pronged pitchfork handle, I shot her a toothy grin. "I've made it this long just fine. What makes you think I can't handle myself on the road?"

Now it was Lettie's turn to grin. "I've patched you up twice. Marge here probably another three or four times. Hell, even Violet saved your scrawny ass once."

I rubbed the sweat away from my brow before starting in on the dirt again. "I could do it you know."

I felt a hand on my arm. Looking back, I noticed Marge there. "Please don't leave," she begged.

That was the problem I had — no way could I counter begging. Nor the tears, acting like I was special or something. My guilt held me back. Well, guilt and a few other things.

Lack of decent footwear was a big problem. Who knew when you had to walk everywhere all the time you'd wear a pair of shoes out in a month or two? Certainly not me. Whatever socks I'd brought, let's just say three pairs, were shot by the time the snows came. Only a stash of six new pairs in Dizzy's shed saved me on that front.

We, Dizzy and I, had yet to set out scavenging the promised cornucopia of places nearby. Something always came up. Something always came up on Dizzy's end at least. And he was always evasive when pressed for a reason. Eventually, he'd toss his hands in the air and walk away. "Just 'cuz," was his only explanation.

But I knew better. Dizzy was sweet on Marge. Now the same couldn't be said about Marge's feelings for Dizzy. But she could play him like a cheap dime store harmonica when it came to getting what she and Lettie wanted done.

My stamina still wasn't good either. Not to make a 400-mile trip, alone much less.

Three hundred and eleven days had passed since the power went out. Well the power, the communications, and the working cars, and basically most of life as I knew it. According to Lettie's scale, I was 41 pounds lighter in that time. Standing naked in my cabin, staring into a full-length mirror, I looked pretty scrawny. I always assumed it was just that mirror.

It would probably take all summer to build my strength enough to make the journey. That would give me the fall to get home. Two, maybe two and a half decent months of weather. But that was only if I was strong enough by the end of August. And each week, I was still losing weight. That was a problem, and I still didn't have a decent solution.

The other thing on my mind, every day now, was the safety of the four at Lettie's place. I had good reason to be worried, though I hadn't shared it with any of them yet.

A few days back, I was north of Lettie's, tracking down a bear Dizzy thought might be in the area. While I had no desire for any more bear meat, Dizzy had other plans. He was going to make sausage.

While he waited at Lettie's place, I went in search of said bear. And I wasn't having any luck finding any signs that he described would mean I was close.

Wandering north still on the blacktop, I noticed a man approaching at a meandering pace. He shot me a smile when he got close enough to notice the 45 in my hand, Frank's old gun that I now carried when hunting.

He took a sip from his canteen, wiping away perspiration that had accumulated on his long, thin, dirty face.

"Howdy," he called out from about 10 yards away.

By this time, I focused on the single man; the bear could wait. While I'd witnessed a number of travelers on the road this early summer, this man didn't look like the rest. Something, somewhere in my gut, told me he was trouble.

"Heading somewhere?" I asked, knowing that Amasa was miles to the south. At his current pace, it might be fall before he ever got close.

"Looking for someone," he replied, offering me his canteen.

I showed him mine and he withdrew it, smiling as he did.

"Looking for a man and his wife, two kids," he continued. My stomach tightened.

"Can't say I've seen anyone like that down this way at all," I lied and something told me he knew I had.

He nodded several times, studying the waves of heat rising from the stint road. "She took something that wasn't hers," he went on, staring at me, seeking a twinge of betrayal. "My boss would really like to have it back."

I considered his vague words. He was trying to draw something out of me. However, I wasn't inclined to bite at his offering.

"She who?" I replied, trying to give him a puzzled expression. One that told him I had no idea what he was after. "The wife or the daughter?"

He took another swig from his canteen and wiped away the excess moisture. His eyes narrowed and focused tightly on my face.

"The wife," he snarled. I couldn't tell if he was upset by the wasted walk or my attitude. I guess I didn't care either.

"If you find a gal named Marge Luke," he continued, "tell her Mr. Callies knows what she did and she needs to return what she took. Got it?" Man, this guy was a jerk. And to think he felt like I gave a crap about his problems.

"Sure," I replied, watching him turn and head back north, towards Covington. "What does she look like, this Marge chick?"

Still walking, he glanced back. "Husband, two kids, 40ish, brownish hair, about 5-6, thin. She's a nurse, too. Just ask names of strangers, okay?"

I nodded, not that he saw. He gave a fairly good description of my friend. Of course, she was missing the husband now, but I still got his message. Marge had their drugs; they wanted them back, and they were willing to travel to make it happen.

Something told me we hadn't seen the last of this guy or his friends.

Day 315 WOP

We worked through the ankle-deep water, my tagalong and me. The water was a shortcut, saving a half-mile backtrack on our snare lines. I didn't mind, but the young man with me hated wet feet.

"I don't have that many pairs of shoes," Nate whined, rapping another tree with his walking stick. "My mom is gonna be mad at me for getting these wet."

Good, since he brought her up, I had my opening.

"How's your mom been lately?" I asked. I moved Nate ahead of me to lift him over a windfall. "She hasn't had much to say the last few times I've seen her."

His frown spoke volumes. "She still cries a lot. Grandma Lettie says she needs to get it all out…even though it's been a while. I miss Dad too, so I don't blame her for crying."

I gave him a soft smile and wrapped my arm around his shoulder. "It's okay to cry, and I miss my dad, too. So, I know how you feel."

"Violet tells me to quit crying like a little boy every time she sees me doing it. She makes me feel bad."

Yeah, unfortunately for him, his sister was 13. And even in

the middle of hell, her teenage mentality came through. Selfish, bitter, needy. A whole bunch of not-so-fun emotions.

"Don't let Violet bother you," I replied, noting a dead rabbit in our nest snare.

It had been Dizzy's idea, the snare lines. Early to midsummer was when does typically dropped their fawns. At first, I thought the man had a big heart, not wanting us to kill a mother while a baby laid in wait for her return.

Then he informed me it was because of the wolves. Hunting deer while wolves hunted the same wasn't a good plan in his experience. If things went badly, they, the wolves, could end up hunting us. Needless to say, I saw his point.

Nate watched me pluck the dead rabbit from the snare and place it in the pack on his back. "I hate cleaning rabbits," he lamented as I pointed him toward the next snare.

"Because they're cute, furry animals?" I asked.

He shook his head. "Nah, because they stink when you clean them."

Yes they did, I thought. But when Lettie made a stew with half a dozen of them, they sure smelled good.

"What do you know about the bad people coming, Nate?"

Shrugging several times, I watched his lips twist. He knew something; he just wasn't a big talker.

He sighed and looked up at me. "I heard Mom and Grandma Lettie talking about it the other night. Grandma said she would shoot them with her gun when they showed up. Mom just cried a bunch. Said she was worried about me and Violet."

"Did your mom say she was sure they were coming?" I know grilling a young child isn't the most honest way of gathering information. I did feel bad, sort of. But my safety might be at issue as well in this situation.

He stopped and looked up at me, all serious and grim. "They're coming," he answered, and then sighed. "And they're coming soon, Mom thinks."

Giving him another smile, I steered him onward. The rotten filth from Covington would come. And I'd have to deal with them one way or another.

Day 318 WOP

Weeding Lettie's massive garden gave me plenty of time alone with her and Marge. Violet, like most young teens, avoided any manual labor at every opportunity. One day her side hurt, a few days later she had a headache. Typical for someone her age when it came to work.

I had sent Nate on a wild goose chase in the bog directly behind Lettie's property. And it was literally chasing wild geese. Stick in hand, the youngster worked at displacing the few Canadian geese we had in the area. If they weren't moved, I'd be standing guard with a shotgun over Lettie's garden. And I had better things to do.

Shortly after lunch, the three of us got back to watering and weeding. We had barely started when Dizzy strolled in with love on his mind. That was fine with me; he needed to be part of this conversation. Whether Marge had any feelings in return for the slightly fitter woodsman was yet to be determined.

Leaning on the shovel, I attempted to ease into the conversation. "Why do you think these people from Covington are coming for you, Marge?" In my defense, my wife had always claimed I wasn't very subtle. But if trouble was coming, I wanted to be ready.

She didn't even look up at me from her weeding. "Because they are," she answered from a kneeling position in the moist, sand-filled dirt. "I believe they are ruthless, and their previous actions showed that."

"So, in round terms, how many drugs did you take?" I continued prodding. "Couple dozen bottles?"

She peeked up briefly. "All of them," she answered blandly. "Everything that fit in a large suitcase. I figured if we were going to be stuck out in the middle of nowhere for the rest of our days, we'd need most of them, eventually."

Okay, her logic made sense. The amount she clipped seemed a little extreme, fairly noticeable. "And what do they want them for again?"

She rose slightly and sat back on her heels. "I've told you this before, Bob. They're going to trade them. By now, there's half a dozen fish camps set up on the shores of Superior. They'll need drugs. I would bet the people in Covington will trade them for some supply of fish."

"That makes sense," Dizzy added, taking a break to wipe his brow with an old stained handkerchief. "We could trade them the drugs back for supplies. That would help us, right?"

Something wasn't right in Dizzy's logic. "I imagine they want them back for their trades," I countered, going back to weeding between short stalks of new sweet corn. "They most likely see them as their property to begin with. So, I don't think they'll be open to trading to get them back."

Lettie reappeared with a water bucket in hand. Before pouring it on the plants, she offered us a cup full each. "When these folks show up, we'll just hide Marge and her family here. Tell them we don't know nothing about any people they're looking for."

I stared back at the older woman in a straw sunhat. "And if they demand to search the place?"

She shrugged, splashing the water in the dirt. "I guess we'll have to settle it with a gunfight."

Her answer seemed too easy to me. We didn't know how many would come, how they'd be armed, and what groups might follow if things got dicey.

I noticed Nate's white t-shirt as he chased through the brush 100 yards or so behind us. That was a good quarter mile short of where the geese actually nested. But that was okay; I just wanted him out of earshot and still close enough to keep an eye on.

"Who's this leader of that group up in Covington?" I asked

Marge, noting Dizzy kneeling beside her, tenderly rubbing her shoulder. Oh, young love…in middle-aged form.

Lettie came closer to me, her face taut with something. "A man named Stuart Callies," she announced in a firm voice. "His kin is over in Iron River. He's the nephew of a rich and powerful man. Well, when money meant something at least."

Letting my eyes settle on hers, I inched closer. "Can he be reasoned with?"

"Not likely," Marge huffed. "The mayor tried to reason with him and that got him hung."

I knelt next to Marge. "They got fire power?"

She nodded. "They showed up with guns of every kind," she answered bitterly. "Most of 'em had a rifle or shotgun of some sort. And almost every person carried a sidearm and a big knife as well. I heard one man got stabbed when he asked a group what they were doing in his driveway."

Okay, well-armed and not the negotiating kind. Two strikes. Add to that the way the man I'd met a while back acted and I felt we had no chance other than hiding our friends.

I rose and glanced at Lettie. "Then I agree with your plan," I said, turning to take out my frustration on the never-ending piles of weeds. "I don't see any other way this works out good for us."

"Staying alive is the main thing here," Lettie called back, heading to get more water. "As if things aren't bad enough, now we gotta deal with a bunch of pukes like that."

I noticed Dizzy wrap his arms around Marge. She was crying.

"I'm so sorry I brought this upon you all," she moaned. "That was never my plan. I just wanted to be safe in the wilderness."

Well, none of us were safe now, Marge, I thought. But that was really beside the point. None of us were safe to begin with.

Day 320 WOP

Two days. Two lousy, stinking days later everything fell to hell. And it caught me completely off guard.

Like the idiot I was deep inside, I walked into a trap that anyone should have seen coming. But not me. No, I was focused on the future.

Dizzy had come up with another bike for me by patching two or three older pieces of crap together. Because his welder still worked, he could modify the front forks on one that was bent. Adding a sturdier pair from a new bike, he even was able to grease the chain and ride it to me. *My escape might happen soon,* I thought.

So there I was, pedaling down the road towards Lettie's at a leisurely pace. I'd just made a quick trip back to my cabin for an axe to take down a tree the old gal wanted gone. Watching the leaves move about in the warm, gentle breeze, I took in as much summer as I could. I knew I had to wait for it to cool down before taking off for Chicago, but while I was here, I wanted to enjoy my tranquility.

Thus, I never saw the man standing on the side of the road. The one with a rifle leveled on my mid-section.

"Mr. Reiniger," he called out, startling me to the point where I dropped the axe. "How nice to see you again. And we have so much to talk about."

Instinctively, I reached behind my back for my pistol. He waved the rifle at me, grinning as he did. "Probably not a good idea," he chided, reaching towards me with his free left hand. "Why don't you just hand me your gun so no one gets hurt, okay?"

No one but me, I imagined he meant.

"Now get off that bike and push it along back to Miss Hamshire's place," he ordered, his face still happy. Why shouldn't he be happy? He had me dead to rights.

We walked the remaining two or three hundred yards and turned into Lettie's gravel driveway. Ahead, next to the shed, I saw my friends lined up. Across from them were three more armed men.

"Just so we're straight on this," the man began again, "this is the woman I was looking for when we first spoke about two weeks ago." He shot me another boyish grin. "But I imagine you knew that, even back then."

"How do you know it's her?" I dared to ask.

One of his men handed him a photograph. "We took this from her home," he answered, handing me the picture. There, all decked out in Christmas attire, was the whole family. And the imprint said it all.

Merry Christmas and Happy New Year from the Lukes: Warren, Marge, Violet and Nathan. Damn, they had her good.

"Now, we have several items that warrant a serious discussion here," he went on. "First," he pointed at Marge, "this woman stole something that wasn't hers, and we want it back. And second, for her crime, she needs to face punishment."

"And you'll be determining that punishment...?" I gave him the same look he was giving me. "I'm sorry; I didn't catch your name."

He shoved his open hand my way. "Matt Weston," he answered in a happy tone. The bastard even gave me a hearty handshake. "These are my boys: Billy, George and Ringo."

None of the three bothered to look back. Instead, they kept the guns leveled on my group.

"Ringo?" I asked. "As in the drummer for The Beatles?"

The man shrugged. "His actual name is Harold, but he prefers Ringo."

"Okay," I began, pointing at my friends. "Maybe if we lower the guns, we can all discuss this civil-like."

"Or," he countered with the tip of his head, "Mrs. Luke

can fetch us those drugs and come along with us back to Covington. That's really the best solution, *Bob*. Leaves the most innocent people unhurt."

Oh, this was a real caring fellow, I could tell. Take Marge back and hang her for protecting her family. And leave the rest of us wondering when they'd show up again for another round of retribution.

"There has to be another way besides taking Marge away," I countered, careful not to sound overly demanding. "I mean, come on; we're all reasonable people here."

His face went sad, almost to the point of a painted circus clown. "Mr. Callies said this is the way it's got to be. So that's what I'm here to do." He slapped my right shoulder, turning me to face him. "You should be happy I'm not dragging your sorry ass back for a lynching. You did lie to me after all." His face returned to its former self quickly. "But you were just protecting the kids, I figure. So no harm with that…for now."

Marge stepped forward in tears. "Please, I'll get you the drugs. And I'll come with you. Just don't hurt anyone else."

In the oddest scene I witnessed in more than 300 days in No Where, Matt opened his arms and hugged Marge. Not a fake little "there, there" hug. No, one where his arms circled just below her shoulders and gently squeezed.

"See," he whispered back to me, "I knew she'd come to her senses."

Like she had a choice.

My eyes drifted to their side arms. All, including Matt, carried 45s; just like the one Frank left for me.

"I got a trade," I announced. "I got a good trade for Marge's safety."

Matt grinned at me one last time. "It had better be one helluva trade there, Bob. Mr. Callies is pretty set on punishing this woman"

Oh, it was. And I bet his boss would love it.

Day 320 - continued - WOP

Matt rubbed his bearded face, considering my trade. Apparently, every man in the apocalypse had given up shaving. However, several of his gang had beards longer than Matt's or mine.

He moved into the shade, away from the hot direct sunlight the rest of us were forced to stand in.

"You want me to take 500 rounds of 45 caliber ammunition in trade for Marge's punishment?" He had it right; that was exactly what I had stated.

"I'll even give you my cart to haul it back in if you want," I said, trying to read his face. A little eye contact might help.

"I think I'm going to need a thousand rounds," he countered. "If you got that much."

A rough calculation told me the going price for Marge's head was $350. At 35 cents a round, based on the last price I ever knew, it was.

My eyes drifted from Matt, to Marge, to Lettie. Her slight nod told me I was on the right path and I should make the trade. But I wanted a little more.

"I get a kicker with that many rounds," I stated, watching

Lettie's face fall. *Have faith, dear woman.* If nothing, I am a great negotiator.

Many was the time I worked a used car sales person down thousands of dollars from the "rock bottom" price. Shelly even refused to go car shopping with me after that first experience. She claimed it was too stressful. Hell, if she had her way, we would've paid $12,000 extra for our house. But I knew how to haggle.

Matt flinched first; excellent. "What kind of kicker we talking about here?"

I moved in for the kill. "We need 50 pounds of salt and at least 300 canning lids," I said, watching Matt's face closely. I could see him considering it, though he tried to act like he wasn't. *The eyes tell all, buddy.*

"Well, salt's five dollars a pound," he stammered, unsure of his numbers. "The lids are another buck a piece."

"Lids are a quarter," Lettie squawked, tossing a hand at the man. "And canning salt is less than a buck a pound. The whole kicker ain't costing you squat. So put that in your pipe and smoke it."

Nodding at her coarse words, Matt looked back at me. "I think we can work out that deal. A thousand rounds of 45 ammo and getting the drugs back will make the boss happy.

Settle the debt free and clear, I figure."

Finally, my breath came easier. "Great, I'll go get you the ammo and you can be gone."

He grabbed my forearm. "Course you got to haul it back to Covington for us and meet with the boss. We ain't hauling no goods back for you."

That made sense. In my haste to get rid of these clowns, I had forgotten how we'd get our supplies.

"Deal," I replied. Two steps and he spoke again.

"And the girl comes with us for insurance," he added. "Just so everything goes nice and smooth."

"You don't need Marge, she's sorry for what she did. But I don't see where hauling her—"

His eyes narrowed. "I meant the girl, Violet," he answered, his voice kept low to show he meant business.

I had intentionally kept my gaze from both kids the entire conversation. I didn't want Matt to think they meant anything to me. They needed to be left out of this.

"No," I answered, watching Matt's grin grow.

He nodded. "Yep. She'll be the family representative. That should make Mr. Callies see the seriousness of your offer."

"Please," Marge begged. A raised hand from Weston quieted her down.

I watched as Violet wrapped her arms over her chest. *Please don't talk*, I begged her in my thoughts.

"I'm not going anywhere with these assholes," Violet spewed. "They can all go to hell."

I closed my eyes tightly, hoping she wouldn't say another word. Yeah, that hope and shit proverb came back to my mind.

"You can shoot me right here," she continued, almost stepping into one of the barrels pointed at her. "Because I'm not leaving." With that, she plopped down in the dusty drive, shaking her head at the group.

"I like her," Matt said, wrapping his arm around my neck. "Mouthy little bitch, full of piss and vinegar. She'll do just fine in keeping us company. Now go get the drugs, the ammo and the cart. Lettie here is going to feed us and give us some water. You got a half hour," he pointed at an old wind-up wristwatch on his arm. "One minute late, and I put a bullet in the boy's head. And we'll still be making that trip."

Day 320 - continued - WOP

Why they didn't follow me around and grab my entire stash of ammunition baffled me. I suppose they thought they were getting it all. If only they knew, or perhaps cared.

As far as Matt Weston knew, he'd hit the jackpot. Not only was he returning with the stolen loot, but he brought gifts as well. I'm sure he expected to be rewarded greatly for his keen bartering skills. We'd see just how Mr. Callies interpreted the deal.

He gave me 30 minutes; I used 22 according to his watch. By the time I had everything loaded and ready, the four men stood in the shade at the far side of the garage.

"Let's get moving," Matt called out, waving Violet and me on. "I want to sleep in my own bed tonight."

I tugged at the cart, the kind with the handle in the front that you had to step into. It would be easier than pushing or pulling single-handedly the entire seven miles. But my cargo wasn't all that light.

One thousand rounds of 45 caliber ammunition had to weigh somewhere near 50 pounds. By itself, that wouldn't have been bad. When I added a large suitcase full of medications, the load easily approached 100 pounds.

The first few miles passed easily. The flat road, lined on each side with trees, provided enough shade to keep the summer sun off our backs. Except for shoes and boots creating road grit, the only sound was the occasional squeak from the cart wheels.

Matt walked on my right, Violet close on my left. Another man with a rifle across his arms led the way. The final two ruffians followed 10 yards behind. Except for those two, no one spoke. And whatever they were saying was low and muted.

"How long you live in Covington?" Matt asked, keeping his eyes ahead.

"I'm from Chicago," I answered, "not here."

I noticed his smirk as he shook off my answer. "I was talking to the girl."

"Lived there all my life," Violet answered, not bothering to look at Matt as she spoke.

"You know a gal named Shalene Sanders?" Matt continued his questions as step after step we moved further away from our homes and safety.

Something in the way he said the girls name bothered me. This wasn't casual conversation in my mind. It was a pointed question.

"I know everyone in Covington," she answered in a snarky tone. Something told me it would have been safer answering no. "She's a couple grades ahead of me, but I know her. Why?"

"Were you still there when her boyfriend killed one of our men?" Matt made death sound like a casual topic of conversation. That made me nervous.

Violet peeked at me. I tried to plead with her with my eyes, but she was going to answer the way she wanted, I knew.

"I heard that guy raped her," she answered bitterly. "Got his throat slit because of it. Seems like he got what he deserved." That last part could have been left unsaid, but not with this gal.

"Well, the details are a little sparse," Matt stated, glancing past me at Violet. "We'd like to find that boyfriend, see what he knows."

This was Violet's opportunity to keep her lips shut. If she couldn't read between the lines here, she didn't need to answer.

"You mean you want to slit his throat or hang him, don't you?" she spewed without so much as a pause. "That's the way Stuart Callies likes to have things done." She peeked his way. "Ain't that right, Mr. Weston?"

I figured he was going to explode, probably chase her down and slap her until she begged him to stop. His face twitched once and then again as he stared ahead at the road.

"He did kill a man," he answered. "Mr. Callies would like to hear his side of the story before he hangs. Rumor has it there was another person with him when he did the deed. We'd sure like to know who that was before he meets his maker."

A 13-year-old without a filter needed to stay out of this conversation. The way I saw it, if she got hung, chances were I was going to hang as well.

I watched as her mouth opened to reply, so I cut her off.

"Now, Violet," I began. "Matt doesn't want to hear all your wild theories about what may or may not have happened with your friends. Don't bother him with heresay and all your personal feelings about it."

Her eyes studied mine and her tanned face did several rounds of contortions as she pondered things. Finally, she shot me a look of supreme anger and went back to staring down the road.

"How much further?" she asked, sounding like a young child bored with a car ride.

"Another couple miles," Matt answered. "There's several hills coming up. So I'll get behind and help push to make them easier. If that's all right with you, Bob?"

That was fine, just great. We'd dodged a bullet in the discussion of Violet's friend. I could tell she all but wanted to admit to her part of the ordeal, either to defend her friends or prove that Matt didn't know everything. With the boyfriend missing, her part in the murder was under wraps.

And we needed to keep Violet out of harm's way at all costs. Even if she didn't seem to see the danger we might be walking into.

Day 320 - continued - WOP

The buildings of Covington came into sight after an hour or so. I don't know what I had expected, but the scene was dismal as we drew closer.

It was as if a low gray cloud hung over the town. Even in the early sunshine, the place appeared dull and dreary. There were homes of yellow, green, and blue, but they all seemed muted. Very few people could be seen out and about. And the small number we did see went about their business without giving us so much as a glance.

Ahead, three armed men blocked the road. Their smiles stood in stark contrast to their surroundings.

"Wondered if you'd be back tonight," a large man toting a sawed-off shotgun shouted. I noticed Matt's grin as he listened.

"Mr. Callies sent me to do a job," he bragged, checking the men at our rear. "When I have a task, I do it right. The boss anywhere close by?"

Another man, shorter and squat shook his head. All three had beards, pretty much like the rest of the male population left in this horrid world. Only Matt's and mine were trimmed.

"He had his supper and retired to his quarters already," the second man informed Matt. "Said he didn't want to be bothered. Something about going over supply lists and such. Sounded important."

The first man struck me as a thug. This man had intelligence in his tone.

"Tell the cook I need two plates of food and a bucket of water sent over to the west jail," Matt announced. Extending his left arm, he pointed west. "You and young Miss Luke will be our guests for the night. In the morning, you can meet with Mr. Callies and finish your deal."

I stopped and rubbed my calloused hands together. Several spots ached with the pain where the rail dug in.

"When do I get my gun back?" I asked, noticing a few more people moving about. Whether they were residents or marauders, I couldn't tell.

"Tomorrow when you leave," Matt replied, coaxing us westward. "I'll hand it to you myself, right at the south entrance. You and Violet and your trade can dance off down the road after that."

He noticed my face, twisted in uneasiness.

"Listen to me, Bob," he continued. "We're putting you up in a jail we don't hardly use. It's for your safety as much as ours. And you don't need a gun any time before you leave. The only people with guns here are Callies people."

He made it sound so nice and neat. Something like *'We'll take care of you, don't you worry about a thing.'* But three things worried me and continued to dog my tired mind.

First, and foremost, who was this Callies character? There was no guarantee that he would take the trade I was offering. Maybe he was driven by revenge. Marge stole from him and needed to pay with her blood and her blood only.

Two of the three men who greeted us carried 45s, just like Matt and his clowns. The gun of choice up here, Frank had told me, is a 45. That's why I thought of offering the valuable ammo as trade. No one was producing any of it any longer, and Covington was miles from the nearest large town.

A second problem we had was our safety. I felt almost confident this group wouldn't harm a young girl. But me? No sure thing there. And if I wasn't around to protect Violet, who would? Matt or Callies himself? At that point, she was a gawky, spindly teen not yet fully blossomed in any way, shape or form. But that could change quickly, as it usually did for teenage girls. An ugly duckling changed into a beautiful swan, sometimes overnight. I had to get her out of here somehow.

Then there was Violet herself. She could be her own worst

enemy here in Covington. Say the wrong thing or get pissed and tell of events that no one else knew and bang, she'd be connected to a murder. If that happened, she could find herself on the end of a rope swinging where the mayor once was. So I needed to impress upon her, when I got the chance alone, to keep her vitriol to herself. At least until we were out of town.

Matt led us to a shed set on the rear of a property on the far west edge of the small town. I could still see the entire community, but this jail was purposely set off by itself.

"It's small and cramped and a little smelly," Matt began, opening the door. "But it should be fine for a few hours. There's a bed and a lawn chair. So one of you can sleep comfortably at least. Food will be here in a few minutes, along with the water. If you need to relieve yourself during the night, just tell a guard and you can go behind the shed."

He must have noticed the question on my lips.

"Yep, even the girl. That's the way it has to be." He stepped inside and continued the tour of the dump. "There's a small window on each end with screens. You should get a little air movement…should."

I noticed clumps of brown grass in a corner where a lawn mower had sat. Birdseed dotted the warped wood floor here and there. An empty tool holder sat in the far corner. Once, not long ago, this was someone's garden shed. Now it was a jail…our accommodations for the night.

Covington was worse than No Where.

Day 320 - continued - WOP

Our dinner consisted of dried beef, perhaps horse, cold carrots and dried fruit that I think were apples. We ate like royalty back home compared to this. Heck, Frank eating a steady diet of pork and beans washed down with generous swigs of brandy was better.

As Violet moaned and groaned about our meal, my mind wandered back to Chicago. Actually, I was transported back to my dream late last winter. The one where I dreamt about grilling out. What I wouldn't give for a decent burger, or brat, or even a hot dog now. Sauerkraut and coleslaw served on the side in Shelly's bright yellow serving dishes. Brownies the size of a dinner plate.

"This is crap," Violet declared, tossing her plate on the wood floor. Her arms circled her waist. "Do you think they'll let me go visit some people tomorrow? I have a couple of friends I'm dying to see."

She opened the door; time to set her straight on the way I saw things. "No chance, not with these folks. They're going to keep a close eye on you no matter where we go."

Running her fingers down the length of her hair, I noticed

her scowl. "Who cares about me?" she vented. "They wanted Mom, mostly. I'm just their insurance policy so you don't go pulling something they don't like."

"You," I pointed a finger at her, "had to open your big mouth about that friend of yours and her killer boyfriend." I lowered myself next to her. We couldn't afford to let our emotions get out of line with guards close by.

"You nearly admitted to knowing what went down," I whispered. "How long you think it will take them to put things together if you say the wrong thing? Maybe they'll just give up on looking for the boyfriend and fit you for a noose in his place."

Her eyes flashed wide. "I didn't kill him," she seethed quietly. Well, as quiet as a teen can be.

"What was your role?"

Trying to shake away the question, she fought my touch when I tried to steer her chin my way.

"I pulled his head back," she admitted, eyeing the windows carefully. It was already dark, but the guards carried kerosene lanterns so they'd be easy to notice. "Jed slit his throat."

Though I should have been shocked that she didn't act more remorseful, she'd been through enough the past year to have a lifetime of misgivings later.

"Do you know where Jed went?" I asked, taking a spot next to her on the bed.

She shook her head at the question. "I don't know. He took off. And I'm glad he did."

"Okay, tomorrow then, you just stay close and keep your mouth shut. Can you do that, Violet? It will make it a lot easier for both of us."

Her lips tightened and she nodded several times.

"Let's get some sleep," I continued. "You lay on the cot and I'll sit over in that chair. Deal?"

Her eyes flashed wildly. "No! You have to sit right next to me on the floor," she demanded. "I need to be able to see you at all times."

Yeah, a scared teen and her unrealistic demands. Just perfect.

"We have a battery powered lantern going in here. You'll be able to see me over there."

She shook off my logic. "Then drag that chair over here, next to me. What happens if the batteries die? Or if they come bursting in here in the middle of the night?" She pulled at the ends of her hair in quick motions. "I want to be able to reach out and touch you if necessary."

She fell asleep holding my hand as I sat in the lawn chair

next to her, as she wished. For me, it was fine. I wasn't scared; I had no reason to be. The worst that could happen to me in the morning was to die. In my mind, that wasn't so bad.

I wasn't afraid to die any longer. Twice, men had tried to kill me. One nearly got me in my own bed. I played with the stub at the end of my left hand, a reminder of how close the second man came.

Chances of getting back to my wife waned with each orange-tinted sunset. The fact I had survived nearly a year was a testament to my friends and neighbors, not my survival skills. Someday I would die out here. If that was tomorrow, so be it. I hoped to live a while longer, but when you have nothing left to live for, then death isn't the worst alternative in life.

Day 321 WOP

Shortly after what looked to be sunrise, the guards brought us breakfast. Hard cooked eggs with a piece of toast each. Both Violet and I had to pick the mold off the edges of the barely browned crusts. Tepid water from last night's bucket helped wash down whatever was caught in our dry throats.

With the new guards sitting on folding chairs before us, they left the shed door open so we could get some fresh air inside. The humidity struck us first; damp air invading our small space. A slight breeze helped cool things a bit, but something told me it was going to be another warm day.

Matt showed up an hour or so after breakfast with two of his three goons in tow. Standing in the doorway, I dared take a step into the dewy grass to greet him.

"Everything ready to go?" I asked, hoping to get things done on my schedule. "I'd like to get back on the road as soon as we can."

Gauging his reaction, something told me *they* had a different plan in mind.

"First thing we need to do is get over to meet the boss," he explained. He stopped beyond the guards, acting as if I might be lethal or something.

"Okay, let's get moving then." I turned to find Violet, already standing next to me, stroking the snarls out of her hair with her boney fingers. "We're ready."

There were small movements in his face as he studied Violet. "She stays, you come."

"Not going to happen, Matt," I answered plainly. "I need to make sure she's safe at all times. That means she needs to stay with me."

He shook away my logic. "No, boss said just you."

Tense moments passed as Matt and I stared at one another. Stroking my beard, I came up with a new tactic.

"Have someone run and get this boss of yours," I stated, seeing the doubt in Matt's eyes. "I need to make sure Violet stays safe. You can't blame me for that."

He glanced at one of his followers and tossed his head back towards the center of town. I was going to meet the boss, on my terms.

What I assumed would take a half hour ended up taking less than five minutes. The guard with saggy blue jeans and a sweat-stained tee shirt had barely disappeared when he came back with another man at his side.

This man was not what I expected. I thought beard, dark clothes, low dipping hat. This was anything but that.

"Mr. Reiniger," the man about my age exclaimed. "Nice to meet you." He extended a hand my way. "I'm Stuart Callies, but please call me Stu. All of my friends do."

I'm not sure what shocked me the most; the clean-shaven face, dark hair cut short and freshly washed? Maybe the baby blue button-down dress shirt, matched with a pair of clean skinny jeans. This was not what I had anticipated for "the boss".

When I stepped out of the shed, I noticed he was shorter than me, substantially. Like six inches or more. Napoleon Bonaparte instantly came to mind. But unlike the dour French general, this man had a charming air about him.

"Bob," I said, shaking his tightly gripped hand. "Bob Reiniger."

His genuine smile, and white sparkling teeth made me feel at ease, but only for a second. A look he gave me told me he was on a mission of some sort.

"I understand we have a question?" he continued, relaxing my hand finally. "How can I help facilitate a solution?"

This was no dummy. And I had miscalculated my opponent. I needed to sober up to the situation at hand.

"They said you wanted to meet with me and me alone," I replied. "I don't want Violet out of my sight, though."

He nodded thoughtfully, even bringing a well-manicured hand to his chin. "I'd like to discuss several things with you, *alone*." He emphasized alone as if it were a coded word. A word that only he and I understood, and I had no idea why.

"You can appreciate where I'm coming from, Stu, can't you?" I hoped by adding his requested name he would see it my way.

"Here's the thing, Bob, I have a certain way I like to do things. It helps this place run smoother." He glanced past me back at Violet. "When people don't follow orders, or simple requests in this case, it makes me edgy. Almost like I can't trust them."

We stared at one another for a brief moment before he continued. "I assure you, with my life if necessary, that no harm will come to the girl. I'll even bring out one of my female soldiers to keep her company if you'd like. But you and I need to talk alone."

I wasn't getting my way, that was for sure. And his veiled threat was plain: we will do this his way.

I gave Violet my full attention. "Are you okay with this? It shouldn't take but a few minutes, maybe an hour?"

The blue shirt appeared at my side. "She has to be fine with this, Bob. She wants you safe, no doubt. You want her safe. And the only way either of you leaves here alive is if we do it my way. So let's go. Cindy will be here in a minute; I've already sent for her."

So much for subtlety on his part.

She nodded once as Stu took my arm and led me away. The fear in her eyes remained locked inside her soul. She wouldn't scream or put up a fuss. His threats made it clear to her how she was expected to act.

I just hoped I could maintain my nerve as well. For her sake.

Day 321 - continued - WOP

He walked briskly. I had to hustle to keep up with the boss. When he looked back to be sure I was following, he smiled broadly.

We passed several people working in a garden. Each just kept at their task, never once looking up at our procession. I noticed they didn't look happy. Hell, they barely looked alive.

The clear blue skies above made it easy for the morning sun to warm us. I was already sweating through my filthy shirt. Stu appeared as cool as could be. No rivets of sweat stained his back, not yet at least.

"We went through what you brought us," he began, slowing so I was at his side. "From what we can tell, most if not all of the drugs are there. And your ammo all seems in order as well. Well played, sir. Very well played."

"All I did was trade a woman's life for a thousand rounds of 45 caliber ammo," I replied, trying not to get sucked into whatever angle he was playing.

"I'm impressed, Bob. Somehow, a mere woodsman like yourself figured out something we'd need." He stopped and turned to face me directly. "I'm shocked actually. How did you know we were short on 45 ammo?"

Fighting back a grin, I gazed down the main street of Covington. Very few people were out, even at the hour. Mostly I noticed armed patrols here and there.

"All four of your posse carried 45s. That told me maybe more of you did." My gaze returned to his smooth face. "I just put two and two together on a hunch, that's all. And I'm not from here, originally. I'm from Chicago."

His smile grew. "I went to school at the University of Minnesota. Just finished my masters there at the Carlson School of Management. Though I hail from Iron River, I had bigger plans. Much bigger plans."

I looked around nodding. "Like taking over a dump like this?" No sense in holding back. This fellow liked to talk.

His laugh came from his belly and lasted several seconds. "Absolutely not," he countered, steering me further down the main drag. "I was headed for New York this fall. About to start my career on Wall Street. Then this," he waved his arms over his head, "whatever this is, happened. But I would be damned if I was going to spend my time playing second fiddle to my uncle back home. No, I was meant to rule."

"So you came here," I said. "Anarchy by opportunity."

He tipped his head slightly. "Some would call it that. But

don't believe all you've been told. True anarchy had begun long before my arrival. Hoarding of limited supplies, letting neighbors starve, and run the risk of freezing to death. Families without any clean drinking water. That, my friend, is truly a lost community."

"So you killed the sheriff and the mayor and made it your own personal slice of hell. I get it. It was there for the taking, right?"

He stopped and pointed at a bench in the shade. I sat and he joined me, our knees almost touching.

"Those were both unfortunate but necessary events. The sheriff and his deputy killed two of mine first. And the mayor threatened us; told us if we didn't leave, he'd have us killed. I knew it was a bluff, but when he came at me with a knife — after I agreed to meet with him alone and speak sensibly with him — well, things had to be done."

I think he wanted me to view him as the savior of the town and its residents. But the two nearby armed guards made that tough to swallow.

"I would have preferred to have Mrs. Luke herself, you understand." His tone was no longer light, but low and solemn. "She's cost me valuable time and resources. She needed to answer for her sins against this place."

"You mean you?" I asked. "She sinned against you, in your mind."

He shook my comment away. "No, I mean the community of Covington. And everyone here."

It was bullshit and we both knew it. But it was better not to call his bluff.

"Do you know the only working vehicle is this place is a late 50s snow plow?" he asked, as if I cared. "That means when we set up our supply line with a large fish camp going up near Marquette, we only had one gas-guzzling vehicle to work with."

"I would think you had some older cars or motorcycles that still worked. Few of those around I bet."

He bristled at my observation. "Anyone who had one of those was gone by the time we showed up. Hell, we walked here ourselves. All 30 of us."

"Why here?" I asked. It was something I had wondered about ever since Warren had told me about this place and its invaders.

"I was born to lead," he replied in a tone of great pride. "That's what I planned on doing in New York, eventually. But the apocalypse had other plans for me. So, instead of sulking and letting my opportunity slip away, I sought out the next best solution."

"But why Covington? There must have been easier, closer spots?"

He shrugged, clapping his hands lightly near his knees.

"After the power went down, my uncle began to employ many locals to serve as his protectors. Food, water, shelter…all guaranteed. Others who wanted to try and make it on their own were on his doorsteps within 60 days. When I mentioned I wanted a key role, he suggested I find that position elsewhere. He has three sons, thus, he didn't need another general."

The way I saw it, this mess was his uncle's fault. At least partially. If only Stuart had stayed put in Ironwood, then this plague would have never happened.

"It's location," he answered in a confident tone. "It's at the center of the route from Ironwood to Marquette. And it's a straight shot south of Iron Mountain. All commerce will flow through here shortly. And when it does, I will be the tax collector."

Shit, this guy knew his stuff. No wonder he was so dangerous.

Day 321 - continued - WOP

I followed Stuart Callies to his office, a neat little place that had once served as the center of government for the sleepy little community, no doubt. Now it was lined with several dozen of the most lost souls I had ever laid eyes upon.

Most wore tattered rags as clothes, with shoes and boots with holes puncturing them. Men with long, stringy hair and longer snarled beards, women with their heads down, hiding their dirty and sunburned faces from my gaze. A few had small children. In the far corner of an anteroom to Stu's office, there was a group of what I assumed were teenagers. They were the only ones talking, leaning near one another sharing whispers. Their eyes held secrets their tongues dared not share.

"These folks are waiting for transport to Marquette," Stu stated, leading me into his large, well-lit office, thanks to many clean, bare windows.

"Looks like they're ready to go."

"Just waiting on my people to pump some gas from the ground," he continued. "That damned truck burns an entire 100-gallon tank going between here and Marquette. We get five gallons at a crack, so it takes a while to fill it. But it will be an even better trip now that Matt has recovered the missing medicine."

I sat back in a luxurious leather chair, hearing the material squeak against my sweaty shirt.

"And what do you get out of the people and the drugs?"

"That should be obvious, Bob. I send them people and supplies; they send us fish in return. Salted and cured whitefish. We've killed just about every living thing within a five-mile radius of town. We're going to need that fish, and soon."

"So you enslave people to the fish camps, and in return, they send you food. Pretty sweet deal, unless you're one of them."

He leaned forward on his elbows against the dark oak desk. "These people will starve here eventually. There, they'll be fed as long as they produce. Some will catch fish, some will clean the fish, others will pack it and cure it. Here, if they can't grow it or kill it, they're of no good to anyone."

"Seems kind of shady to me," I said dryly. A young woman, as clean and bright as Stu came in and served us cool lemonade. When she turned to leave, I noticed her white sundress covered in smaller red flowers, perhaps roses. How out of place these two appeared.

"I know you don't see me as a modern day savior to these people, but it really is better than the alternative they faced without me. At least I have a plan. I know how to obtain and utilize resources. The people in charge before me were dolts. By now, there'd only be a handful of people left alive in Covington. Under my guidance, our population has remained steady in the low 300s."

I sat forward, staring into his medium blue eyes. "Here's the bottom line. I don't give a shit about any of this. I struck a deal with your man, and I expect that deal to be honored. So give me the salt and lids and my gun back, and we can part ways."

He nodded thoughtfully at my demands. At any moment, I expected him to open a drawer, take out a gun, and shoot me smack dab in the middle of my forehead.

"You're going to need to be a little more patient, Bob. You see, I have a very limited supply of salt at this time. I can't spare 50 pounds."

Okay, this wasn't good, but it was workable.

"What do you say you give me back 300 rounds of ammo and we'll call it even then?" Hell, he wasn't the only negotiator in the room.

His sour expression told me he didn't like my counter-proposal.

"When the truck comes back from Marquette later this evening, I'll have the salt. If you don't want to wait that long, that's fine with me." His eyes narrowed to the size of almonds. I wasn't going to like what he had to say next. "But I'm not giving up any of that ammunition now that it's here. So you'll just go home with a box of canning lids and whatever's left of your pride."

"That's not what Matt and I agreed—"

"Matt doesn't have a final say in negotiations," he interrupted loudly. "I, and I alone, make the final call. I wanted Marge Luke back here. I could have sent her to a fish camp and received her weight in fish every year for the few pitiful years she'd last."

His rant caught me off guard. Thus far, he'd been calm and polite. But, like with most narcissists, his mood flipped whenever he didn't get his way.

"I'd rather know that a thief received her just reward than have something I could just take from you," he continued, calming with each word. "But I'm a gentleman and a man of my word, even when given by others. So, you and young Miss Luke are safe as long as you are my guests. You'll receive plenty of lids and a generous amount of salt. But not until it arrives later tonight. You will be my guests again. And we'll all get through this ordeal in one piece. I trust I'm being reasonable enough for you?"

He was the man in control. He was the one with the guards. Smart to separate Violet and me, he proved his true intentions. As long as every detail went the way he desired, everyone would he happy. And by everyone, he meant himself and himself alone.

"I trust you can wait…Bob?"

I nodded. Like I had a choice. He had other plans, but I had no idea what they were. But something told me I wouldn't be in the dark for long.

He snapped and pointed at one of the guards. Immediately, the older man with the sawed-off 12-gauge left the room.

Yeah, I wasn't going to have to wait too long.

Day 321 - continued - WOP

The bastard had Violet brought to us, and that made me nervous. So far, as much as I knew, she'd kept her mouth shut. I wondered how long that would continue once Stuart Callies began in on her.

The self-appointed leader excused himself and left the room with all of his people following. The double doors were closed and I heard them walk away on the hardwood floor. Only then did I glance at the girl.

"Well?" she demanded, giving me a look of supreme anger.

"There's a delay," I answered, reaching to pat her hands on her lap. "We have to wait for the salt to arrive tonight sometime. I think we'll have to stay one more night in our quaint accommodations."

"That's just great," she snapped, slapping my hand away. "And you believe him. The man who kills people just for fun."

I knew she wouldn't be thrilled at the news, so her reaction was about what I expected. Pushing away from her chair, she began to pace behind me.

"This is bullshit!" she seethed. "We should have just let them kill us all in Grandma Lettie's driveway. It would have saved us a long walk to our deaths."

I needed to slow her wrath down. Maybe a little logic would help. "I don't think he plans on hurting us, Violet. Actually, I believe his story about the salt."

Her eyes rolled one way as her head lolled the opposite. "Wow, you are stupid aren't you? They never intended to trade us anything. Why can't you see that?"

"That doesn't make sense, Violet. If anything, these people of his have been decent to us. Hell, even Callies himself has acted anything but severe. I think he wants the trade as much as we do."

"He does." Another voice entered the discussion from behind, causing Violet and me to jump. It was the woman in the white sundress.

"If you two would come with me," she offered, opening the doors fully as she spoke. "I'll take you to a room where you can get cleaned up a little."

"I don't want to clean up," Violet countered with a dash of spite. "I want to go home, to my mother."

The woman smiled broadly and nodded. "And you will. All in good time. Just follow me please."

Waving us forward, I had to push gently on Violet's shoulders to get her to move. She looked up at me timidly, fright blanketing her face.

"Don't worry," I whispered. "I got your back."

We moved as one, Violet grasping my hand tightly with both of hers. As we followed Susan out of the office, I wondered if anyone had *my* back.

We were led out through the same hall I entered, still full of the same lifeless lot that originally greeted me. Out the front door, the woman turned right and peeked back at us.

"This way," she said in a cheery voice as if she were leading a field trip at the zoo.

Pausing ever so slightly, I studied our surroundings. No guards bothered to follow us. The two at the end of the street behind us disappeared around the corner of a building, not giving us a second glance. Ahead, a few townsfolk staggered in our direction, heads down, hands in their pockets as they passed. I almost ran into someone. It was her again.

"If you want to run off…" she stated tersely, "…go ahead. You won't have your lids or salt. No one will give you back your gun or your wagon. But no one will stop you either."

My confused look made her smile, a little.

"What exactly don't you understand?" she asked. "What was it that my brother told you that didn't make sense?

Perhaps I can clear it up."

First off, I didn't know they were brother and sister. But that really didn't matter at that point. "Where are you taking us? And what's going on?"

She waved for us to follow again. "I'm taking you to a room where you can clean up and put on some fresh clothes. You both look like you've seen better days; I thought it was the least we could do for you while you're delayed."

Ah, her idea. He was the monster, she was her brother's keeper…or attendant…or soul.

"We're going to have a nice lunch in a little bit," she continued as we entered the building next door. It was completely devoid of people, making it feel a bit creepy. "We've rigged up a fairly decent shower in here. There's a large basin that has warm water, enough for both of you. There's soap and shampoo. Even nice clean towels to use when you're done."

I grabbed her arm, spinning her to face us. "Why are you doing this?" I demanded. My eyes searched for any treachery in hers.

"Because we're not bad people, Mr. Reiniger," she implored. "Apart from what you may have heard about Stuart, he's not an evil person. He is trying to help."

"Could've fooled me," Violet inserted, tipping her head to the right. "He's killed plenty, I was here. One of his men tried to rape my friend. Sounds evil to me."

"And that man was punished," the woman responded quickly. The slight lines on her face told me she was Stuart's older sister. Spread amongst her auburn hair a few sprigs of gray showed through. "I knew you think things were all right here before we showed up. But they weren't. No small town would last without food, fresh water, basic supplies, and a plan."

Violet stepped closer to argue with her. "I just don't think —"

The woman reached and stroked Violet's dirty face. "You're such a beautiful child," she cooed, wiping a smudge of dirt away. "This world has turned our lives upside down, and in an instant. One moment we were watching TV, chatting on our phones and computers. Then, so quickly, everything turned ugly."

Violet's expression softened hearing the sincere words from another.

"When Matt and I arrived, we told my brother the only way we'd help is if we did things the right way," she said, turning her attention to me. "I'm Susan Weston; Matt's my husband. Stuart sent for us last winter. Said he needed our help. Help doesn't include starving, or raping, or killing. Help means compassion."

"Well, you're a real angel of mercy then," I said, perhaps a little sarcastic. But from what I'd seen thus far, Covington wasn't a very compassionate place.

"I don't expect you to believe me," Susan went on. "Not with the history that Violet and her family have told you. But give it a chance, give us a chance. And you'll see. This isn't a bad place, and we're not bad people."

I shrugged and she led us deeper into the building. The jury was still out on this place, and these people. All of these people.

Day 321 - continued - WOP

She led us up a tight stairway and onto the second floor. There, in a small room, was the shower she promised. On a desk outside the bathroom door sat clean clothes for each of us.

"I guessed at your sizes," she offered, patting the clothes. "They may be a little large, but they're cleaner than what you have on. The door locks, so you'll be safe." She stepped closer to Violet. "And no one will enter this building while you're in here. You have my word."

Violet nodded once, swallowing hard. I knew she was skeptical; hell, I was skeptical. It all seemed too good to be true.

"There's a toothbrush for each of you in there." Susan pointed into the steamy room. "And some powder that I hope you find refreshing. When you're both done, go back downstairs and into the building we just left. Someone will lead you to the dining hall. We have a nice lunch prepared, and I'll be sure it's kept warm until you join Stuart and I."

The slap of her sandals disappeared slowly as she left us and descended the stairway. I listened and heard the front door snap shut.

Glancing back at Violet, I saw her fear rising.

"I don't trust her," she said, pulling on her lower lip. "I don't know what she's up to, but I don't trust this whole place."

I turned her for the bathroom, handing her a pile of women's clothing as she entered.

"Neither do I," I stated, reaching to pull the door shut. "But I really want a shower. Don't you?"

Studying the room, she shrugged several times. "Okay, but you stay by the door. Don't leave me."

I found a chair and sat it in front of the door, protecting my friend. I wasn't going anywhere. I was about to have my first shower in almost a month. Wild horses couldn't drag me away from that chance.

Clean and freshly dressed, Violet and I made our way out of the building. Standing on the shaded sidewalk, I watched as she flipped her long, wet hair several times.

"What I wouldn't give for a blow dryer," she commented, following me back to the first building.

"What I wouldn't give for one of Lettie's brownies right now," I replied, leading her past the single female armed guard by the front door. "I'm so hungry, I could eat dirt."

She stopped me by jerking at my arm. Her eyes darted around the room, checking for danger, I assumed.

"Just be careful," she whispered. "They might try to poison us. Maybe we should tell them to trade plates once we're served."

Laughing away her fear, I urged her forward. I had noticed Susan waiting on the far end of a hall when we first walked in, so I figured the food was in that direction.

"We'll just watch them take the first bites," I said, mostly to myself. I don't think Violet was listening all that closely. However, I doubted I would be waiting for anyone else to begin eating, not with the amount of growling my stomach was doing.

Baked chicken, mashed potatoes with butter melting on the top and bright orange carrots adorned the center of the table. I winked at Violet. If they were trying to kill us, we'd all be dying.

A beautiful white linen cloth covered the large oval table, making me pause before I sat. The dichotomy of our surroundings was pronounced. Outside, people worked in the sun, dirty and hungry. They struggled each day for another meal, another sip of water. Inside was a world from almost a year back. All existing in the same place, changed by the unknown.

"Tell me, Stu," I began after taking a large bite from a greasy chicken thigh. "What happened late last summer? What caused our world to become like this?"

Wiping his mouth first, he posed for his answer. "I have several theories, and none of them involve the worn-out idea of an EMP attack."

I glanced at him, confused. "Why not an EMP attack? Seems like the most logical choice."

He shook his head. "A man came through Ironwood several months after the attack, shortly before I came here. Riding an ancient motorcycle from the 50s. He was from the southwest somewhere. Arizona, New Mexico; makes no difference. He said it was the same down there. Shortly after we arrived here, a group of travelers came through headed west. They came from somewhere in southern Ontario, over near Sudbury. Same thing there."

Well, he had half of North America covered. That would have been a number of high-level EMPs. That seemed unlikely.

"If you ask me," he continued, "and you have, I say it was high-intensity solar flares. Something in the magnitude we've never experienced before."

I nod while taking a large spoonful of potatoes, the butter coating my tongue. Up until that moment, I had no idea how much I'd missed that one dairy product.

"Where do you get butter from?" I asked, licking the back of my spoon to get every last drip.

I saw Susan dab at the corners of her mouth with her white linen napkin. "We have a woman with a small herd of cattle. We agreed to protect her property and she graciously offered to provide us with milk and butter. She has some chickens as well. Quite a few actually. Thus, our noontime feast."

"Would you like to hear my other theory, Bob?" Stuart begged for my attention from the other end of the table. I shot him a small smile. There was something about these two that didn't make sense.

"Aliens!" he shouted. Like a child at a carnival, his face exploded with glee. "Someone from a far off distant galaxy has other plans for our world. Throwing us back into the dark ages was just the first step."

A fist pounded the table at the other end. "Stuart!" Susan cried out. "Please stop with you childish thinking. Our guests don't want to listen to such drivel. Be an adult."

His face shrank along with his shoulders. Going back to his

plate, I watched him pick at his carrots with his fork.

"You'll have to excuse my brother," Susan apologized. "Sometimes he lets his brilliant mind wander to places that it doesn't belong." She set her hands in front of her face. "Say, how would you both like to stay with Matt and I tonight? You don't deserve to waste your time in that horrid place my brother insisted you stay in last night. Wouldn't nice soft beds with clean sheets be better?"

I nodded blankly. What didn't make sense before became clearer in my mind. Both of these people were trouble. But who was running this place: brother or sister? Which one was our real enemy?

Day 321 - continued - WOP

"Maybe you're not listening, or maybe you're just too stupid to see what's going on!" Violet shouted, taking aim at me once again. "There is something really weird about these two. And we shouldn't trust them at all. I say we leave now and forget about the salt."

Lunch was over and Susan encouraged Violet and I to take a stroll around town. Stuart didn't seem happy with the idea at first, but it grew on him when my teen traveler asked if we could go visit her old house.

For some reason, one thing that almost floored me most as we excused ourselves was we were allowed to roam freely... sans guards. But I knew people would still be keeping an eye on us.

Violet led the way, and within minutes, we stood in her parents' former living room. Most of the house had been thoroughly searched I could tell, most likely looking for the missing drugs. If they had left any food behind, Violet couldn't recall, it was gone now. Even the beds and linens had been removed.

A newer TV sat on the far wall, the one without a window.

Fifty inches, I thought. Would have been pretty cool to flip it on, cop a squat on the couch, and watch a couple innings of the Cubs, but we didn't have the time. Nor the electricity or any more sports teams probably.

"What's freaking you out?" I asked, watching her twist her fingers through her hair. The girl was going to have massive snarls if her anxiety didn't get under control soon.

She glared at me as if I were the dense one. "He's a freak and a killer. I don't care what he says; everyone at the bar that night said he killed the sheriff. A friend of mine watched the mayor get hung. And they said Callies laughed the whole time." She started pacing again, working the length of the 20-foot room. Something she had probably done in the past.

"And what's with that sister of his?" she shot at me, along with a light arm punch on one of her passes. "I mean, she seems nice, but so did Dotty's mom. Dotty was one of my friends."

The tale stopped too quickly. She stared blankly at me.

"What happened with your friend's mom? Finish the story."

"Oh yeah," she said. "Well, one night her mom found out her dad was cheating on her. So she took the kids, cut all their hair off, shoved them in a car, and made them watch her burn their house down. She was crazy. She got busted, of course, but she was nuts."

Strolling to the front window, I stared at the vacant streets. No one seemed to live on this end of town, the south side. I rubbed my forehead, wondering if Violet was losing it.

"That's a delightful story, Violet," I began in a somewhat mocking tone. "Not that it has a single thing to do with our current situation." I turned and faced her again. "Does it?"

She hustled straight at me. "Dotty's mom was beautiful, sweet, well-respected, adored by all." She snapped her fingers in front of my eyes. "And just like that, she went bat shit crazy."

"I'm lost here. Just who do you think is crazy?"

Violet's eyes shot open wide. "Both of them," she vented. "There's something not right with either of them. And one of them's gonna blow. I think it's the woman. We spend the night at her place, tomorrow morning she wants me to call her momma — or some crazy shit like that — and the next thing you know, we're all dressed up playing rich crazy people right alongside of them."

Holding my chin so my mouth wouldn't drop open, I nodded thoughtfully, several times, many times actually. "Have you ever been diagnosed with some sort of overactive imagination kind of thing? Maybe something that goes along with your anxiety."

She walked away, shaking her head. "She'll probably cut your nuts off, make you one of them kind of servants. Give her baths and shit."

"A eunuch?" I asked, wondering how she came up with some of this stuff. "Don't you want to find some kind of memento to take back with you? Something you didn't have time to grab before?"

"I'm not like that," she answered blandly, her face becoming emotionless. I'd seen this look before.

"There must be something here you want. Maybe a picture or something that reminds you of your dad."

"I don't want to remember my dad," she answered hastily. "And I don't want to talk about this no more. We need to leave."

She was out the front door so fast, I had yet to push off the comfy couch. I found her throwing rocks from the gravel driveway into the backyard.

"You don't know me," she continued without looking back. "I know you don't like me, and I don't care. And you know nothing about my family or what I need."

Okay, she was 13 and prone to fits of self-pity. That much came with the territory. And I really didn't go out of my way to spend any time with her. Most of our encounters were of the forced variety, à la getting my finger shot off. But that didn't mean I didn't like her…most of the time.

"I like you just fine, Violet. And I know you've been through a lot. And you miss your dad—"

"You don't know nothing about nothing, do you?"

I tried to get her attention, but she ignored me by spinning away. "Tell me something about yourself you think I'll find interesting. Try me, you might like me." Her head spun and she glared at me. I gave her a smile.

She spiked a small rock past me, thumping it into the side of her former home. Her lips twitched, her eyes narrowed. We were perhaps at a breakthrough moment.

"My dad was mean to me and my mom. Just words, but he was awful," she confessed. Her tone sounded like casual conversation. Something like *'the weather is so nice today.'* "He'd get mad about something and start in on us. Make us cry. Tell us he was going to leave us both. Just take Nate and leave us to the wolves."

She shuffled on the porch. "First time it happened I was scared, real scared. I thought Mom and I would starve to death. I was only seven. Then, the more it happened, the more I prayed it would stop. By the end, I wanted him to leave. Just so he'd quit telling me and Mom how worthless we were. I never knew when it was coming, but once it started, he just kept going, and going, and going. Not until me and Mom were on our knees in tears, begging him to stay, did he stop."

"I'm sorry," I whispered. What a lame response on my part.

"We didn't talk about it much because he always promised afterwards he wouldn't do it again."

Her eyes showed none of the pain I expected. This had been going on a while, I was afraid. And for a moment, just a flicker of a heartbeat, my blood ran cold.

Day 321 - continued - WOP

"When my dad got that cut on his leg, the one that got all infected," she continued, taking a seat on the corner of the small front porch. "My mom had me empty all the medication out of the pills before we gave it to him." She looked up and shrugged. "He was in a lot of pain before he died. He begged us, with tears in his eyes, for more medication. And we kept feeding him those empty pills, one after another."

Her admission was painful, for me. Not so much for her.

"He caused us enough pain, all because he had a bad temper. Mom tried to get us help once. They talked to him and told us to work it out. Probably wasn't as bad as it seemed, they said. When I killed that man on the road, it was like I was shooting him."

I tried to part my tight lips, but they were stuck and dry. I don't know medically what you'd call Violet, or even Marge for that matter. But I knew what they went through wasn't good.

"That man, Stuart Callies," she made eye contact briefly, "he's got a lot of my dad in him. Seems all nice to everyone, but he's waiting to explode."

"And his sister?" I asked.

She nodded, scratching at the side of her face. "That's my mom, waiting for revenge. But probably not on her brother. There's something in her past. And if you've lived a day like that, you can see it. I can at least."

Carefully, I took a spot next to her. There were no tears on Violet's face. But the lump in my throat made it hard to speak.

"I'm sorry for what you had to go through," I said. "I didn't know."

Cocking her head, she looked at me seriously. "I'm 13 and my life is shit. First my dad, then the world, then a bunch of strangers. It's not fair. It just ain't fair."

She sighed. "I want a normal life, that's all I want. But people just keep messing with me. I thought maybe after Dad passed it could be calm. But here I am again, stuck in the middle of a situation where my brain tells me we're in trouble."

I laid my hand on top of hers. Once upon a time, I was a teen. But not like Violet. I remember one time at 14 not being allowed to take the L with my friends to a game. I thought my world was over. That was nothing compared to a single moment in her life.

"Let's just be really careful," I managed, sounding terribly inept. "Let's agree to watch each other's back, and listen to what the other has to say. Let's get out of here safe and sound and get home. Okay?"

She was quiet for a long while. Something else was going through her mind.

"Sometimes I wish I was dead," she admitted. "Maybe all this pain would be gone."

Her words hit me hard, real hard. I fought the tears back. Slowly I wrapped my arm across her thin shoulders, squeezing her lightly.

"I'm so glad you're alive and here with me, Violet. I'm happy to have you, and your mom, and Nate, and all the others in my life."

"But you're gonna leave, aren't you?"

Finally, the truth came out. I had known this young girl for almost six months and for all of that time, she looked at me with extreme hatred. Now I knew why.

"You're nice to me," she stated in a quiet tone. "Dizzy's nice to me and he makes my mom happy. I don't want you to leave. You keep the bad people away."

Tears streaked my cheeks. Maybe it was the thought of home, so far away, almost unreachable. More likely, it was the fact that I was wanted, needed. Even in a place I hardly considered home.

I was the guy with a temper when I arrived in No Where. But fear, followed by a desire to stay alive, took away all of my wrath. I had never so much as struck another human being before I came here. Now, I had killed two men, men who wanted to kill me.

The remorse sometimes became unbearable when I was alone at night. I wept for the souls I extinguished. But in the light of day, in the eyes of a young teen, I had found the truth.

I wasn't a monster. I was a survivor, a protector. And I was needed.

Now it was time for my own moment of truth.

Day 321 - continued - WOP

It would hurt to say it aloud, but Violet had already displayed what pain looked like when set free. If she could admit that her life wasn't perfect — or anywhere near that — then I could as well.

"I'm never getting back to Chicago," I admitted, forcing the words from my lips. "I'm never going to see my wife again. Not my mom or my dad, my brother. None of them."

I noticed her look up at me from the corner of my eye. There was more.

"I don't like killing people, but I don't want to die. The first man," I shot her a look to see if she was still watching me. She was. "The first man made me throw up afterwards. Didn't have a choice, though. The second guy, that meant nothing to me. I just waited too long before pulling the trigger."

"He shot your finger off," Violet added, reaching for the stub on the end of my left hand. It was covered in scar tissue and still looked bad. "You were protecting me."

"Was I?" I made direct eye contact with her, and she shrugged. It was my question after all. "Or was I just pissed at the world, like you, and wanted to take it out on someone? I don't know."

"What are you going to do for a woman if you stay?" she asked, changing the subject away from its depressing course. "Mom has Dizzy, Lettie's too old for you, I'm too young. Aren't you gonna be lonely?"

Funny, in all this time, I'd never thought of another woman other than Shelly. My memory of her waned with each passing day, but until now, I'd never given up hope of getting back to her. Her face, her smile, her laugh, her charm faded more, becoming only a distant memory, like a dream of something I never had.

"I'll be fine," I answered, trying to smile. "I've got to get back to liking me before I can like someone else."

"Maybe someone will come along."

A small laugh came out of my mouth. "Yeah, maybe. But for now, we need to concentrate on getting back home in one piece."

She sat up on her knees and leaned close. She placed a small kiss on my cheek. "I'm glad you're my friend, Bob."

I looked at Violet closely. And for a moment, I felt good inside. For a brief time, the world seemed all right.

"I'm glad we're friends, too," I said, giving her a small hug. "Neither of us are perfect, and that's okay. We're fine though.

Just fine."

For the next half hour or so, Violet and I sat on the porch. Neither said much. What more was there to say? The world was an awful place. Both of us were stuck in the middle of No Where, almost against our wills. But we had family — well, she had family — and good friends and a place to call home. If that's all we could have at this time, that was all right, too.

Down the road, I spied a man in a bright green tank top and shorts coming our way. It didn't take long to recognize him.

He waved and called out our names, happy to see us.

"What do you suppose Mr. Crazy wants now?" Violet asked as we rose from our spots.

I didn't know, but at his quick pace, we'd find out soon enough.

"I was hoping I'd find you here," Stuart announced with a grin. "Won't be but two or three hours and the truck will be back."

Violet and I met him in the dead grass in her former front yard. He was dripping with sweat.

"I was just out for my afternoon walk and thought I'd track you down. I have a proposal for you, both of you actually."

I hadn't noticed before, but this guy was ripped. He had the whole package: abs, bulging arms and legs of steel. Muscles bulged, covered in a thin sheen of moisture. His arms and legs were tan, dark brown like his face. *Where was this guy finding time to work out and tan in the middle of an apocalypse?* I wondered.

Steering us towards the road, we walked with him — albeit at a slower pace than when he approached.

I decided to strike first with my questions. "If that truck gets back before dinner time, we could leave and make it back home before dark, right?"

He nodded, pushing his short dark hair back on his forehead. "True, but if you had any trouble, you'd be stranded between here and there in the dark. And I know from my group that there's been a lot of wolf sightings down that way lately. So I'd prefer, for your safety of course, that you leave tomorrow morning after breakfast."

"We haven't seen many wolves," Violet said matter-of-factly, sounding non-confrontational for a change.

"You probably haven't been out much at dusk though, have you?" Man, this guy had an answer for everything.

"That's when the wolves are at their best," Stuart continued, almost enthusiastically. "They have such an advantage over us mere humans at night. I'm afraid they'd make quick work of you."

I glanced at Violet, who seemed unmoved by his speech, but it had my attention. Their nightly baying had been increasing all summer. We were, back home at least, surrounded by them.

"I guess we wouldn't be averse to staying," I admitted. "Depending on when that truck gets back..." Violet jabbed at my ribs to let me know her dissatisfaction. However, based on our chat over the past hour, I was thinking of her safety, as well as mine.

Stuart clapped his hands loudly. "Excellent! I'll let the cook know to expect two more for dinner then." He began to trot away, but stopped and spun to face us. "By the way, Susan is looking for you both. She's downtown where we had lunch. I believe she has some refreshments prepared."

With that, he jogged away. Just like a normal person would during the summer. If the world as we knew it hadn't ended a little less than a year ago.

Day 321 - continued - WOP

We found Susan lounging outside the building downtown, just as we were told. She motioned for us to join her on the old wooden park bench set back in the shade to keep away the warm summer sun.

"Please, join me," she called in a sweet voice. "I've some lemonade made with cool well water. I think you'll like it. Violet, sit on my left so I can be in between you two."

We sat as instructed and the promised beverage was delivered to us immediately. Susan smiled, chasing her long auburn hair away from her collar.

"How'd you find your home?" she asked Violet, clutching at her hands like a caring mother.

She shrugged. "About the same," she answered in a pouty tone. "Seems like most of our stuff is missing."

Nodding at the words, Susan raised Violet's chin so they were face to face.

"Most of it was traded," Susan answered. "For food and fish. Anyone who left made themselves open to these types of actions."

"Stuart's idea?" I asked.

Turning, she smiled graciously at me. "Yes, it was. And I must say, I approve. We're going to need plenty of food here in Covington when winter comes. And any trades we can make with new communities will be vital."

"How many fish camps are being set up?" I meant to ask this before.

"I'd have to check with my brother for the accurate number, but I know of six or seven at this time. Several have been extremely productive so far. Harvests have been good. Given what little they have to work with."

I grinned and leaned back against the wood slats. "Let me guess: small boats, large nets, some might have motors, others just oars. Probably fishing from sunrise to sunset, seven days a week. Women and children cleaning and preserving the fish."

Again she smiled and I found it, and her, attractive. Still, I knew deep down she was dangerous. Stuart Callies was her brother after all.

"I really wouldn't know, Bob," she replied, almost sounding bored. "The whole adventure is quite barbaric and smells to high heaven in my mind. So I'm avoiding going anywhere near any of those places. I prefer the quiet life here in Covington."

She slipped an arm around Violet's shoulder as they both

sipped their drinks. While on the surface her actions appeared innocent enough, my gut did backflips watching her pay attention to the teen.

"Is most of the killing done, now that you're here?" The question slipped out of my mouth as a reaction to her actions. I watched Susan's eyes closely as she turned.

"My brother has promised me that he would treat people with more respect now," she answered, seeming to take no offense to my blunt question. "People are dying of starvation, but we have no hand in that. It's of their own choosing."

"You could give them some of your food," Violet retorted snottily. "You seem to have plenty."

Susan turned and took Violet's hands again. "Listen to me, Violet. There's an important lesson for you here. My brother, my husband, all of their people are working so hard to make this a sustainable community. Everyone has to do their part. But some people…"

Susan reached out and squeezed Violet's face to turn her head back to facing hers. "Some people take advantage of us. We allow them the latitude to harvest their own crops. Half is for the community, and they can keep or trade the other half. Yet, when we go and inspect their shelves, do you know what we find?"

Violet shook her head slightly. I could tell by her expression that she was scared. "Sometimes they give us a third of their bounty. Sometimes not even a quarter. Now I ask you, where is their sense of community? Where is their love for their fellow man? How can we feed those who aide and protect them if we aren't given our share?"

"I don't know," Violet squeaked.

"We don't kill them for their transgressions any longer, Violet. But they are punished. And yes, sometimes we may make a larger example out of one of two of them, but it's for the good of the community in the end."

I watched as Susan waited for the teen to digest her diatribe. And what a load of crap it was. If Violet was expected to buy that fairy tale, we'd be here another week before it sank in.

"Which brings me to another topic," Susan added, straightening her sundress. "Matt didn't have a chance to inventory all of the pills before we had to ship them off. But he did make a quick list so we can match it against the inventory sheets."

She had my attention. She also had the full container of pills, according to Marge.

"Brought you back everything Marge took," I stated, noting

her sweet expression was gone and replaced with a semi-scowl. "She may have used some items for her family, but everything else should be there."

Susan raised a hand. "I have no issue with the woman taking care of her family. I'd do the same for my own. Matt mentioned though it appeared we were still missing a number of bottles, perhaps penicillin and some other painkillers. Might you know anything about that, Mr. Reiniger?"

I shook my head honestly. "Absolutely not."

"How about you, dear?" Her eyes were back on Violet.

I saw the flash right before the eruption came. "I don't know nothing about your stupid pills," she shouted, slapping at Susan. "My mom gave them all back to you just like that piece of shit husband of yours—"

Susan grabbed a handful of hair and pulled back. Her face changed so much I hardly recognized her. Her eyes small, lips tight.

"Listen to me and listen to me good," Susan spewed at Violet. "I was 13 once and you had better believe I was never allowed to speak with an adult in that tone you just used. I expect you to behave like a proper young lady while you're here. If you want to act like a piece of gutter trash elsewhere, then be my guest. But not in my home."

She released her hair and stroked Violet's tear-streaked face. "I'm sorry," she whispered. "But I expect more from you." She turned and faced me. "Both of you."

Guards were close enough to keep my rising anger in check. But they sure didn't seem taken aback by Susan's rant.

"I got no idea what you mean, lady. I just want to get this trade over with so the girl and I can get back. Really, that's our only purpose here."

Susan sat quietly, tapping her lips with her left index finger. There was more, and her evil dark eyes foretold of something I wasn't going to like.

Day 321 - continued - WOP

"I want to speak honestly with you," Susan began, her face tight, her body rigid. "With both of you. So listen carefully to what I have to say."

I noticed Violet roll her eyes behind Susan, and I fought back a grin.

"I appreciate honesty. And if you two are being honest with me, then we have no problems." Susan paused, glancing at me, then Violet. "But I won't tolerate lies."

She stood and began to pace in front of us. I slid closer to Violet.

"If I find out either of you has lied to me about your knowledge of any missing drugs, there will be serious repercussions. Am I understood?"

I nodded, but Violet ignored her. Susan reached and clutched the teen by her cheeks, jerking her eyes up to hers. I saw the nails of the other woman digging into my friend's face, causing little red indents. Before I said something I might regret, I noticed a guard had slipped in closer, so I resisted.

"Listen to me you little bitch," Susan seethed. "When I find out you've lied to me, either of you, I will bring you back here, dragging you by your hair if I have to. Then I will hurt you, both of you, badly."

She knelt in front of the shaking girl. "I will hurt you in ways you never imagined possible. I will have you begging me to stop. By the end, you'll beg to die. But I won't do that.

"No, I'm going to tie you to a chair, as battered and bruised as you'll be. I'll glue your eyelids open if I have to. I'll make you watch me hurt your friend here in ways that will shock your mind. You won't ever forget the things I do, because they'll be that evil. If you think you've ever felt pain before…"

She laughed manically in Violet's face. "When I'm done with him, then I'm going to come back to you, little girl. And I'm going to hurt you more. I'm going to keep at it until your voice gives out. And only when your screams become little squeaks will I stop."

Glancing back at me, Susan continued. "If you two get back there and find any of the missing drugs, I expect you to turn around and immediately bring them to me. I want you to walk her barefoot to show me your contrition. If you think about running and hiding, I will find you. And my wrath will be twice as bad."

She rose and wrapped her arms over her waist. "I trust my honest conversation has gotten through to both of you?"

I nodded. "Absolutely."

"Yes, ma'am," Violet answered quietly.

"I don't want to be this way," Susan admitted. "But if it's the only way we can keep order, I trust you understand."

She turned and left. Violet refused to look at me as I watched Susan disappear down the street. I had my answer. Both brother and sister were just as bad as the other.

"Told you she was crazy," Violet spit in my direction, some of her normal disdain resurfacing.

"Sounds to me like she's a lot like your dad was," I said, sliding next to her. "Maybe not the lopping off of body parts she implied, but the words at least."

"Where are we going to stay tonight? She'll kill us if we stay at her place."

She had a point. I no longer trusted Mrs. Weston or her brother. Either could snap and we'd just be two of the poor souls who "didn't understand how things worked," in Covington at least.

Dinner was a quiet affair. Except for the clinking of silverware on plates and the occasional question that was answered promptly and politely, not many other sounds filled the dining room. All throughout our tenderloin, new potato and asparagus meal, Violet and I shared nervous glances.

When the subject of sleeping arrangements arose, I stated we'd prefer to stay in the shed again. Though Susan glared at me while I spoke, she knew why. I'd seen her fangs and didn't want to risk her bite.

A guard followed us back to our accommodations; I guess our carefree unwatched time was over. By the shed, we found Matt waiting for us with my loaded cart nearby.

"Everything's here," he stated, pounding on the large bags of salt. He lifted the lids and let the bag crash into the cart, just to prove to me that they were there.

"I'll give you back your gun in the morning at the same place you came into town," he continued. "I'll have the cook pack some toast and jam for you, maybe even a canteen of water. You'll want to be on the road right away I bet."

Opening the door, the heat of the day rushed from the shed. That was okay; I couldn't imagine much sleep. Violet neither I assumed.

"Susan talk to you about the missing drugs?" he asked.

"*Alleged* missing drugs?" I countered. "As far as we know, you got everything. If we discover different, we'll get them up here right away."

Sighing, he looked away. "Don't be a hard ass about this,

Bob. If that lady didn't send them all, we need them. And it's best you bring them to us, rather than making us come get them. That'll just piss Stu and Susan off royally. And neither of us wants that."

"But if you got everything already, then this over, right? You'll leave us alone."

He nodded several times before strolling away. "You'll never see us again, most likely. Just be sure we got everything. That's the only safe play." He waved. "Sleep tight; see you both in the morning."

The guard followed him, leaving Violet and me truly alone.

"I hate this place," Violet said from behind. "Even more than when I lived here."

"Well, hopefully we're never coming back, right?" I turned to see here glaring at me.

"Is that a wish or a promise?" she asked. "I kind of need to know."

"I have no idea, Violet. Only your mother holds the answer to that question."

She turned and plopped on the single bed, patting the place next to her spot for me to join her.

"So, what are you thinking?" she asked, lying down, shoving the pillow under her head.

A small chuckle came before my words. "I really hate this place, too. Probably as much as you do."

She smiled, closing her eyes, grasping for my hand. "I told you this was a bad place," she said, yawning.

I watched as she drifted away for the night. Her tiny mouth opened slightly, easy breaths came and went. Perhaps her dreams would be pleasant. Maybe, if she was lucky, she'd be like me most nights and no dreams at all would disturb her sleep.

Day 322 WOP

We left without issue the following morning. Just after sunup, Violet and I retrieved my 45 from Matt. Retreating down the highway, south towards home, I was glad to leave Covington behind. The place was a dump run by a foul crowd and I didn't want to return anytime in the near future.

The seven miles home went by quickly. Violet even took a few tries at pulling the cart, mostly on level ground or when we came to a slight down slope. I figured at our leisurely pace, we'd be back at Lettie's well before noon.

Just past midway, Violet (in the lead at the time) stopped and pointed into the brush just off the left shoulder. Watching carefully, I noticed the leaves and stalks move. Four pups leaped out onto the road.

"Cuuute!" she squealed, looking back at me. They were cute, and furry and some sort of large breed, I figured.

She turned and took a step when I noticed the brush move again.

"Stop," I whispered as loudly and severely as I dared.

Mid-stride, she glared back at me. "Why?" she demanded in a typical teenaged tone. "I want to go play with them."

The look on my face must have been enough to give her pause. Slowly, I pointed as the mother lumbered onto the road.

"Those aren't dogs, Violet," I whispered. Moving sloth-like, I stepped forward and pulled her close to me as the mother barred her canines at us. A guttural growl followed as she moved toward her pups.

I felt the teenager tremble as I moved her cautiously behind my body. The female wolf studied our shapes and movements, her eyes alert for any sign of danger.

I slipped my gun from my waistband and checked the chamber. Still loaded, good. Carefully, I released the magazine and examined it.

Bone dry.

"Shit," I muttered, checking the wolves again. "I hope this doesn't get too dicey. Those bastards emptied my magazine. I got one shot."

Violet's slim arms wrapped tightly around my waist. Her trembling was now an all-out shaking. Glancing at my knees, I expected the same. I was happy to find I was standing firmly.

"Maybe you won't have to shoot." The voice behind me was so small, I almost couldn't believe it was the same young woman who made such a stink in Covington.

Minutes crept by. The mother tried to corral her young and chase them off the road several times. If it hadn't been such a tense standoff, the scene would have been idyllic.

Finally, the group disappeared in the brush on the opposite side of the road. I counted to 500 twice, just to be sure they were gone. And finally, I pried the pair of arms from around my waist and got Violet on my side.

Hand in hand, pulling the cart with my waist, we inched forward, passing the spot where we last saw the wolves. Keeping an eye on our back trail, we hustled another few hundred yards down the road before we slowed.

"That was scary," Violet admitted with another whisper, looking back one last time. She gripped my hand tighter. "I'll be glad to get home."

I looked at her, giving her a soft smile. "Me too." I was through with this mess.

Lettie treated us to a celebratory dinner. I suppose we deserved one. After all, we had successfully maneuvered the threats known as Stuart Callies and Covington. We also managed to get home in one piece. The salt and the canning lids were a bonus. I hadn't really expected to get the deal done, but here we were — fat and happy, sans the fat.

A venison meatloaf sat in the center of the table. On one side was a bowl of boiled new potatoes (last year's), steaming as the late day sunshine lit the room. Green beans and a loaf of freshly baked bread sat on the opposite side. The only thing missing (in my mind) was a full slab of butter. I imagined it would be a while until I saw that again.

"Where's Dizzy?" I asked as we passed the serving plates around the table.

Marge gave me a smile. "He got hot on some big sunfish he told me about at breakfast. He wanted as many as he could get, given we had salt coming to treat them with. He'll be back later."

That darn Dizzy, I thought. Even in the middle of his newfound love with Marge, he just couldn't resist the chance to be outdoors…and alone. At least he was happy.

After the meal was over, Lettie cleared the table while the wash water warmed on the wood cook stove. Questions about the trip were held until the meal was over. Though I expected many, especially from Marge, one thing was forefront on her mind.

"So, how was Covington?" she asked, folding her hands on the table. I could tell by the look on her face she expected the worst.

"Just as dull as ever," Violet answered. I don't think that's what her mom was after.

Marge rose from the table and shooed the kids into Lettie's living room to play a board game. When she returned, she sat and stared at me.

I sighed, considering my words. "It's in bad shape, to be honest about it." I paused to gauge Marge's reaction. Her nod signaled me to continue.

"Callies runs the place with a velvet iron fist. Sure, he comes across as nice, almost sincere. But all problems are dealt with swiftly and harshly. He doesn't always just kill the offenders. He seems to be big on public humiliation and degradation. Now his sister and her husband are there as well. I'm not sure which one is worse. Stuart plays the role of leader, dishing out orders.

"Susan seems to call a lot of the shots from behind the scenes. Tries to come off as all prim and proper, but I ain't buying whatever she's selling. And if they keep selling people to the fish camps, their group will be the only ones left in Covington come next spring." I noticed both Lettie and Marge staring at their laps as I spoke. The answer wasn't happy and light, but neither were the conditions in Covington.

Sitting in silence, only an occasional deep sigh filled the

room. Even the two in the other room played their game in relative silence. With great internal debate, I decided to leave the question of the missing drugs for another time, perhaps when Marge and I were alone.

"Do you think they'll be back?" Lettie asked.

I nodded, if only to myself. "Yeah, I don't think we've seen the last of Callies or his men." The truth seemed bleak, almost as if our future held no hope, but it needed to be said.

I noticed Marge look up. "And what will we do when that happens?" Her eyes appeared tired, as if she'd seen enough of this apocalypse. I felt the same.

That was the question to end all questions. When, not if, they returned, how we would handle it?

"We'll have to fight," I admitted, my voice soft, yet sharp with a need to survive. A year ago, this all would have been foreign to me. Dealing with people who desired everything we had. People who would come and take what little we had left, by force if necessary. Now it was my new reality…our new world.

"Can we win that fight?" Marge asked, her voice trembling slightly.

"We have to," Lettie stated. She straightened in her chair. "It's our survival we're talking about. And I'm not ready to give up yet."

She was right. We'd stand, and we'd fight. And if that meant killing every last one of them, then so be it.

#####

Thank you for reading my latest creation.

If you enjoyed *Stranded No Where*, please consider going to Amazon and leaving a review.

I appreciate your support.

e a lake

Other Books by e a lake

This is e a lake's entire book library at the time of publication, but more book will be coming out in the near future. Find out **EVERY** time lake releases something by going to ealake.com/contact and filling out the contact form at the bottom of the page. In the comment box, simply state "Add me to your email list." Sign up today; all people on my list are eligible for my monthly prize drawings.

WWIV - In The Beginning

WWIV - Hope in the Darkness

WWIV - Basin of Secrets

❖ ❖ ❖

WWIV - Darkness Descends (The Shorts - Book One)

WWIV - Darkness's Children (The Shorts - Book Two)

Coming Soon:

Surviving No Where (Book 2)

About the Author

e a lake and his wife reside in Woodbury, MN; just a mere ten minutes from downtown St. Paul. He has three grown children (all married), and four grandchildren.

Sign up for lake's newsletter at: ealake.com/newsletter

Follow lake's weekly blog at: http://ealake.blogspot.com

Follow lake on Social Media:

Twitter - @ealake5
Facebook - ealake5
Google+ - +EALake

Thank you for reading my novel.

Made in the USA
Middletown, DE
19 May 2020